loss of sense of

'"It doesn't happen here" is a [...] have heard in church, and [...] Writing from a Christian faith-based perspective Sally provides bite-sized information about abuse and how to move forward. It also provides space for reflection and action. This is a practical book that enables both survivors of abuse and their friends and family to work through what has or is happening to them. It is an important read that could be lifesaving to one of your friends and family. Buy it, no buy two – one for yourself and one for your friend.'
Mandy Marshall, Co-Founder of Restored and Director for Gender Justice – Anglican Alliance

'Clearly and sensitively written, this book is a trauma-informed and pastorally sensitive workbook for Christian women experiencing domestic abuse. Combining sound practical advice with gentle biblical application, it will help to equip and resource survivors and those seeking to help them.'
Helen Paynter, Director of the Centre for the Study of Bible and Violence and author of *The Bible Doesn't Tell Me So: Why you don't have to submit to domestic abuse and coercive control*

'I'm so delighted that Sally has created this journal out of her brilliant Always Hopeful course. This journal will not only illuminate the path to recovery from domestic abuse, but help women discover they have the strength to walk it.'
Bekah Legg, CEO, Restored

'I had the privilege of taking part in an Always Hopeful course a year ago and benefited greatly from Sally's work as I made steps in my own recovery. Her new book will surely be a similarly supportive friend for other survivors navigating their healing without a support group. *No Visible Scars* is richly shaped by Sally's own personal experience as well as extensive research and as such is hugely informative and thought-provoking. And yet it also retains its commitment to openness, giving space for survivors to reflect on questions for themselves and come to their own conclusions.'

Becky, Survivor

'A practical and reflective self-help book, written from the heart to support women of Christian faith navigate themselves through their journey of domestic abuse and beyond.'

Karen Allen, Regional Safeguarding Manager and Co-Chair, Methodist Church Domestic Abuse Steering Group

'*No Visible Scars* is an excellent Christian resource for those who have experienced Domestic Abuse; it is so refreshing to see a book that not only doesn't shy away from the difficult conversations about God's response to Domestic Abuse but also allows women affected to explore those challenging questions safely.

Sally brings a genuine and authentic reflection of her own lived experience with such refreshing honesty. This can only encourage other survivors to feel safe enough to continue or, indeed, to take the first courageous step into exploring their own lived experience with the hope that it can support them to live the abundant life that God promised them.

"I have come that they may have life, and have it to the full." John 10:10 NIV.'

Sarah Coates, Domestic Abuse Response Coordinator, The Salvation Army

'Over the past 10 years of supporting women on their journey to healing from domestic abuse, we've seen firsthand the unique struggles Christian survivors face. Many were unable to fully engage in therapeutic support because they were consumed with fear – fear that leaving their abusive partner meant they were failing God or risking eternal punishment. The weaponisation of scripture and the lack of understanding from faith communities created deep barriers to healing.

This book is a vital resource in breaking down those barriers. By grounding real survivor experiences in faith and offering a compassionate, scripturally sound path to healing, *No Visible Scars* gives Christian women the clarity, support and hope they need. Survivors' voices must be heard – not only to help them reclaim their lives but to raise awareness, reach others in similar situations, and drive meaningful change.

This is not just a book for survivors – it is also essential reading for churches and faith leaders. Many well-meaning church communities lack the knowledge to support survivors effectively, sometimes causing further harm despite their best intentions. *No Visible Scars* offers valuable insight into the challenges survivors face and how churches can become places of refuge rather than sources of shame.

This is an important and long-overdue resource that should be widely available and actively used to support Christian survivors and educate faith communities alike.'
Robyn Riggans, Founder & CEO, WORTH (Women On the Road To Healing)

'This book is a much-needed breath of fresh air. It fills the gap for Christian survivors of domestic abuse and digs into what the Bible really says about abuse, dispelling the myths and rhetoric women in Church often absorb. Most importantly it gives hope for a future, free from abuse and a hope that ultimately rests in Jesus.'
Becky Barlow, CEO, Beauty for Ashes Refuges

NO VISIBLE SCARS

An Always Hopeful guide to healing
from domestic abuse as a Christian

Sally Hope

First published in Great Britain in 2025

SPCK
SPCK Group
Studio 101
The Record Hall
16–16A Baldwin's Gardens
London EC1N 7RJ
www.spckpublishing.co.uk

EU GPSR Authorised Representative
LOGOS EUROPE, 9 rue Nicolas Poussin, 17000, LA ROCHELLE, France
E-mail: Contact@logoseurope.eu

British Library Cataloguing-in-Publication Data
A catalogue record for this book is available from the British Library

ISBN 978–0–281–09106–5
eBook ISBN 978–0–281–09107–2

1 3 5 7 9 10 8 6 4 2

Typeset by Fakenham Prepress Solutions
First printed in Great Britain by Clays Ltd

Produced on paper from sustainable sources

helpful, gentle format
short chapters, lots of
blank space — more workbook
5

Contents

Contents

Introduction

My memory no longer functions well, but I still remember that moment, standing in my kitchen, the cord from my landline phone wrapped around my waist, the old-fashioned handset pressed to my ear. I was explaining to my sister why I'd asked my husband to leave. I vividly remember her saying, 'That's domestic abuse.'

It may have been the first time I fully recognised what I had been experiencing. A week later I left a meeting with a Women's Aid support worker, stunned; I'd expected her to tell me to stop wasting her time – she had *real* domestic abuse victims to care for. Instead she told me that the risk assessment she'd just carried out suggested I was in danger of homicide, and she needed to put measures in place to increase my safety.

I'd spent sixteen years with my husband, but it wasn't until after I left him that I acknowledged I was a victim of domestic abuse. This was because I had a whole set of preconceptions about what domestic abuse looked like and what a domestic abuse victim looked like. As far as I was concerned, I did not fit that stereotype. Many of us find it difficult to acknowledge that what we have been experiencing is abuse; it can feel like an overreaction or as though we are 'playing the victim'. In fact, many of us will be accused of doing so, not only by our abusers, but by a society that is still largely ignorant about the dynamics of an abusive relationship and the trauma that is caused by living in one.

Perhaps you're also confused about whether what you experienced was domestic abuse. Maybe you prefer to think of that relationship as 'unhealthy' or 'toxic'. That's OK. Maybe you still love the person who hurt you, or maybe you're wrestling with anger and contempt. That's OK. Maybe you're flipping between feelings of love and hatred and that's leaving you feeling confused too. That's OK. Everything you feel about what you have experienced is valid. There is no right way to 'be a victim'. If you don't want to consider yourself a victim, that's OK too. I didn't either.

Chapter 2 of this book delves into the definition of abuse in further detail, and if you're struggling to understand your experience, it may offer some clarification. Whether you end up identifying your relationship as abusive or not, if you have been in a relationship that has left you wondering who you are; that has impacted your faith, made you uncertain of where God is, or made you question whether you're good enough for God, then this book is for you. If a relationship has hurt you, left you feeling broken; if it has dented or even destroyed your self-esteem and sense of worth, then this book is for you. If you can't make sense of your feelings, if you aren't sure whether it's OK to get divorced, or leave, or move on, then this book is for you.

It's possible that you're wondering, 'Am I even a Christian any more?' That's OK too. Abuse challenges faith; it leaves us with questions and doubts. Things we were once certain of become difficult for us to continue believing. Our experiences may have disproved some of the beliefs we once held dear, and this can leave us shaken. When what we believe changes, it can be frightening, as it forms a huge part of our identity. More than that, for many of us our faith is our salvation, so losing any part of it can make us feel doomed. Please be assured, you are not saved through your own human, fallible ability to believe, but through the faithfulness of Christ. Even if you can't hold on to that right now, don't worry. Jesus can hold on for both of you.

If that last sentence is something you're not sure you believe, that's OK too. There are no creeds in this book, no doctrines you must believe in order to benefit from it. If you feel your faith is in tatters because of your experience of abuse, then this book is for you.

After leaving my meeting with Women's Aid, I began the arduous journey of my own recovery. I slowly unpeeled the layers of religion that had kept me in that dangerous situation, all because I was scared of letting God down. For a long time, I thought I would lose my faith completely, but God had other ideas.

Domestic abuse is isolating, and for Christian women perhaps even more so. We imagine domestic abuse doesn't happen to Christian women. Only two in seven[1] Christians believe their church is equipped to handle a disclosure of domestic abuse. For those of us who do disclose, we often find that support is lacking because our churches don't understand what we are going through.

Domestic abuse affects Christian women at similar rates to their non-Christian counterparts. We just don't talk

---

1 Free resource, 'In Churches Too: Key findings', available at: www.restored-uk.org/about/our-research/ (accessed 29 November 2024).

about it. Rather, it is shrouded in silence and stigma and shame. Meanwhile, secular support agencies are not equipped to handle the questions about our faith: Does God really hate divorce? Why didn't God protect me? Did this happen because I didn't have enough faith? Do I have to forgive? Is my anger sinful? And the list goes on.

After navigating my own recovery and rebuilding my faith, I became a group recovery practitioner, helping other women rebuild lives free of domestic abuse. Recognising the need for a recovery programme specifically for Christian women, I pooled my training, my professional experience and my personal journey to create Always Hopeful: an eleven-week programme specifically for Christian women who have experienced abuse. If you are able to join an Always Hopeful programme, I don't think there is any substitute for journeying with other women who get it, as you can encourage and be encouraged by them along the way.

That said, there may be any number of reasons why you would prefer to read through a book in your own time rather than attend a group session. Perhaps you don't yet feel confident enough to join a group and would prefer to make that journey alone in the privacy of your own thoughts. Or it may simply be that you just can't find a programme near you that you can attend. That's why this book is important. It makes the content of Always Hopeful available in the form of an individual workbook. By working your way through this book, you will undertake your own journey of recovery as you also figure out your walk with Jesus. This is not a companion guide for the group programme but a standalone recovery book for anyone to make use of, whether they have attended group recovery programmes or not. This isn't a traditional book; it's your unique journal, so please don't keep it pristine. Write in it, draw in it, highlight parts that speak to you, doodle in the margins – make it your own. This work is no longer mine; it's yours.

Get messy

How it works

The book is divided into ten chapters and each chapter has two smaller bite-sized sections. In each section, as well as information and tips, you will find questions for you to consider, with space for journalling and a suggestion of something you can do for yourself. The 'to do' tasks are varied, and some will resonate with you more than others, but I'd recommend pushing yourself to have a go at some of the ones that don't feel as comfortable to you.

Between the chapters you will find five Bible studies that consider themes and ideas that may have been weaponised against you. There is no one Christian consensus on the interpretation of most of these passages, though wherever you fall theologically, there is no room for domestic abuse in any biblical understanding. Domestic abuse is thoroughly unacceptable to God. This book does not aim to provide all the answers, but instead to be a springboard for you to 'work out your own salvation with fear and trembling' (Philippians 2:12).[2]

---

2 The word translated 'fear' here may be more accurately translated as 'awe'. We are not supposed to be frightened of God, but we should be awestruck by God's magnificence.

The sections headed 'In her words' contain real quotes from other Christian women, just like you, who have lived through domestic abuse and survived. I hope you find encouragement in these words. And for those who like to study and go deeper, there is a list of recommended reading at the end of this book, most of which has been inspirational to me. All the Bible quotes throughout this book are taken from the NRSVA (New Revised Standard Version, Anglican Edition) unless otherwise stated. You may also notice as you read through this book that I have chosen to use gender neutral pronouns for God. Sometimes, when we have experienced abuse at the hands of a male person, it can be unhelpful for us to use male language for God. God is neither a man nor a woman. God is God and transcends our understanding of gender, and I feel language that reflects this can be more useful when we have experienced a gendered crime.

In a similar vein, throughout the book I often refer to perpetrators as 'he/him'. This reflects the fact that the majority of perpetrators of domestic abuse are male.[3] However, I acknowledge that abuse happens in same-sex relationships as well and hope that anyone with a female or non-binary perpetrator is able to read beyond the linguistic style. I also acknowledge that men can be victims of domestic abuse too, but this book speaks exclusively to the female experience.

---

3 Domestic abuse-related prosecutions in the UK during the year ending March 2020 were recorded as 92% male (ONS, 2020). You can read more about the gendered nature of domestic abuse at: https://www.womensaid.org.uk/information-support/what-is-domestic-abuse/domestic-abuse-is-a-gendered-crime (accessed 18 December 2024).

To do

Before you embark on your journey, it can be helpful to assess where you are right now. When you have finished this book, you can repeat this assessment to see how far you have come. It also helps you to consider which areas of your life you need to focus on.

Think about each of these areas and give it a score out of 10 based on how you think it's going. Then add the scores together to give yourself an overall total out of 90 (or 80 if you don't have children).

Education, work and learning ☐
Support networks and relationships ☐
Health and well-being ☐
Happiness levels ☐
My spiritual life/relationship with God ☐
Feeling safe from abuse ☐
Finances ☐
Confidence and self-esteem ☐
My ability to parent my children well (if relevant) ☐

Total score ☐

On the following pages are some tips for your support network about supporting survivors of abuse. You may wish to cut these pages out and pass them on to your friends and family.

To friends and family

You may have picked up this book to give to a friend or family member who is experiencing domestic abuse. Or perhaps a survivor has passed these pages on to you to help you better understand where she's coming from.

If you are a concerned friend wanting to help, then thank you. Thank you for caring, for taking action and for recognising that abuse isn't just a private matter, but a social one that we all have a responsibility to address. Even if doing so can feel scary, the Bible tells us to seek justice, defend the oppressed, take up the cause of the fatherless and plead the case of the widow (see Isaiah 1:17). Domestic abuse is one of the biggest injustices women face today, and we all have a biblical responsibility to defend those affected by it.

It can be difficult to know where to start though, can't it? No doubt those outside of the relationship, looking in, can feel a sense of powerlessness and helplessness, and fear that they are only going to make things worse. Please don't be deterred, however. Let me offer my tips for supporting victims and survivors of domestic abuse.

Safety always comes first

Even if she has left the abusive relationship, don't assume that she is now safe. In fact, the most dangerous time for a woman in an abusive relationship is when she leaves. Abusers often maintain a hold over their victims for some time after the relationship has ended, especially when there are children involved.

If you have bought this book with the intention of giving it to her, you may want to ask her if it is safe for her to take it. If her abuser sees she is reading a book about domestic abuse, it could put her in further danger. Consider asking if she needs you to store it for her and offer her a safe place to come to read.

Remember that she has been living with this danger for some time, so she is the expert in her own safety. Ask her what she needs. Does she need you to help keep a log of abusive incidents and store that securely away from her home? Does she need a safe place she can go to if she feels she is in danger? Does she need a codeword she can say if she wants you to call the police? Is it safe for you to ring or text her, or do you need to let her take the initiative with communication? Be proactive in asking her. Do not confront the perpetrator, as this is likely to put her in further danger.

Respect her journey

No two people's experiences of domestic abuse look the same, and no two people's paths out of it are the same either. Many women in abusive relationships do not recognise what they are experiencing as abuse. So if you've bought this book because you have concerns for a friend, be aware that it may not be received well if she has not yet acknowledged the abuse herself.

Sometimes women in abusive relationships cope by becoming defensive of their abuser, so tread carefully and don't use pejorative language when you talk about him, as this may only serve to alienate her. On the other hand, if she has recognised the abuse, she may be extremely angry and feel hatred towards him. Please don't judge her for this or tell her she needs to forgive him. Working through our feelings takes time and is all part of the process and journey of recovering from abuse.

Respect her choices

On average, a woman will leave her abuser eight times before she leaves for good. It can be very frustrating to watch a friend return to an abusive relationship, but as with acknowledging the abuse and dealing with our feelings, this is part of the process. It could be deciding whether to stay or leave, or whether or not to report it to the police, or anything else, but her choices are hers and hers alone. While it can cause us to feel hopeless to see someone making what we believe are bad choices, it is important that we respect this and allow her to make her decisions herself, because abuse disempowers victims. If we try to persuade or coerce her into different choices, we are behaving like her abuser.

Keep records of abusive incidents

It can be difficult for survivors to remember everything that has happened to them. Trauma has physical effects on the brain and can cause memory problems. It will probably be unsafe for her to keep records, and when she is in the abusive relationship, she may not want to anyway. Often survivors choose to report the abuse a long time after the incidents. Any records you keep could be valuable evidence. Be careful with what you record and where you store it. Use initials rather than full names, and keep your record factual. Do not add your own judgements or opinions.

Name the abuse

The longer we live with abusive behaviours, the more normal they become to us. This is one of the reasons why many women in abusive relationships don't realise it's abuse and don't leave; it has become their normal. By naming the behaviour as abuse, telling her it's not acceptable, and most importantly saying that she doesn't deserve it, you can begin to counter some of the messages from the abuser.

Give her a self-esteem boost and remind her who she is

Abuse erodes our identity. Many of us, when leaving abusive relationships, feel as though we simply don't know who we are any more. Abusers use a variety of tactics to make their victims feel small. One of the key factors in helping women to leave and recover from abuse is a strong sense of identity and improved self-esteem. Anything you can do to remind her she is loved, and worthy of love, will help. She is God's precious daughter.

Provide community and support networks

Psychologists have identified a number of factors that increase women's resilience, helping them to cope when they live with abuse and recover better when they leave. These factors include having a strong sense of community and good support networks. This is an area where churches and Christians should be able to excel. Try inviting her to community events, social events, church groups and so on to help her feel part of her community.

Don't discourage her questions

Traumatic events such as domestic abuse can trigger periods of deconstruction. Deconstruction is the act of taking an inventory of our beliefs, looking at each one in turn to assess whether it is still valid and helpful. Deconstruction can be scary, because we invest so much of who we are in our belief systems. However, it is also a perfectly normal and healthy thing to experience. If questions and doubts are met with rigidity and disapproval, the person deconstructing is more likely to lose their faith altogether. It is better to meet questions and doubts with openness and honesty, encouraging her to work out her own faith and to trust Jesus to keep hold of her heart as she does so.

Persevere

A common tactic of abusers is to isolate their victims, and they will often do whatever they can to drive a wedge between them and their friends and family. He may tell you tall tales about her; he may have told her lies about you; he may have sown seeds of distrust among you.

And it's not just when she is in the abusive relationship that abuse can cause problems for friendships. Trauma can make us behave in odd ways, even as we move beyond it. The effects can be long lasting. You might find that your friend pushes you away as you attempt to help her. Be aware of this and try not to take negative behaviour personally. Rather, be quick to forgive. Even if you have to remain at a distance for her safety or your own, be ready to step back into the friendship when you can.

Love

It can feel overwhelming when a friend or family member faces a problem as significant as abuse. We can feel as though we're not qualified or adequately resourced to offer the help she needs. Don't try to do everything. Instead, encourage your friend to seek help from professional domestic abuse services. If you are in the UK, the number for the National Domestic Abuse Helpline is 0808 2000 247. If you are elsewhere, you should be able to find your own country's helpline with a Google search. Those charities can signpost you to the relevant services in your area.

But while you may not have all the qualifications to offer the best practical and legal help, and while you may not have all the answers, you are infinitely qualified and resourced to offer her what she needs more than anything else: love.

Abuse claims to be love. It masquerades as love, but it is not. Abuse is the antithesis of love. Those of us who have been exposed to abuse need more than anything to be exposed to an abundance of love. Don't worry about what you don't know and what you can't do. Just go out there and be Jesus to your friend, because that's what she needs the most.

1

A new hope

Section 1: From hopeful to hopeless

Hope deferred makes the heart sick, but a desire fulfilled is a tree of life.
(Proverbs 13:12)

Before we begin, I'd like to tell you a little of my own story:

As I tugged on my battered Doc Martens and tied my purple laces I was filled with hope and excitement. Today I was piling boxes of my old life into my dad's car and heading off to uni to start a new one. I had plans, big plans: get a degree and then become an actress. I believed I could do anything and my future looked rosy.

And then I fell in love.

As my new husband carried me over the threshold into our new house, I felt so grown up. I had a home, a job and a gorgeous husband. I was filled with hope and excitement about the family I'd raise; I had even designed the nursery for the spare room.

I had many hopes over the next thirteen and a half years:

- *I hoped he'd be in a good mood.*
- *I hoped he'd keep a job.*

- *I hoped the next job/house move/hobby/friendship would finally make him happy and contented.*
- *I hoped he'd get the psychiatric help he needed, so he would stop having 'anger issues'.*
- *I hoped he'd get justice for the things he'd suffered that had made him this way.*
- *I hoped the responsibility of children would change him.*
- *I hoped the children wouldn't be damaged by how he treated them.*
- *I hoped the children wouldn't see how he treated me as an example of how they should treat me, or their wives when they grew up.*
- *I hoped, most of all, that God would fix him.*

Then one day I gave up hope and left him. I felt utterly hopeless. I couldn't imagine a future without him in it and I no longer felt I could do anything. I had no dreams or ambitions for myself, because I'd given them up long ago to pursue someone else's dreams.

Over time I have learned to be hopeful again. But now my hope is not in a fallible human being to treat me how I deserve to be treated, or to take care of me. My hope now is in Christ.

My misplaced hope in my husband led me only to disappointment, but I know that Christ will never disappoint me. I can have a future without my husband in it. I can have a future not dependent on any man. I'm God's daughter – he loves me, he wants me to grow and flourish, and I'm learning to stand in that hope.

Do you identify with any part of this story? Take a moment to note down what you relate to.

Proverbs 13:12 tells us that 'hope deferred makes the heart sick'. For many who have experienced domestic abuse, this is only too familiar. We continually hope that things will change; that this isn't the real him; that one day we will have the future and the family we imagined. It doesn't seem too much to hope for really: a normal family, a contented marriage, a husband who loves God and loves me. Yet, as time goes by, our hope goes unfulfilled, our heart becomes sick, and we can be left wondering, 'Where is God in all this?'

Over the next ten chapters we're going to consider that question. We'll examine God's attitude to abuse, to divorce, to women and to men. We'll think about why God didn't change our abuser, why God allowed it to happen and what this might mean for our future faith. But we will start by thinking about hope.

To consider

Take a moment to think about your own hopes.

A new hope

What did you hope for when you were younger?

What did you hope for while you were experiencing abuse?

What, if anything, do you hope for now?

A new hope

What is the difference between a hope and a wish?

When you thought about the last question, perhaps you decided that a hope is something tangible and realistic. The things we wish for are not likely to happen, whereas a hope is something we can believe in, because it is possible. Our hopes are created by evidence. For example, a student who works hard under a committed and faithful teacher can hope for good exam results, whereas a lazy student with an inconsistent teacher can only wish for success.

Abusers are not capable of fulfilling the hopes we place in them. In reality those hopes are wishes, but most of us do not realise this until we are free of the abuse.

Take a look at the diagram on the next page. This is one model used for understanding abusive relationships. It is limited, because not everybody experiences domestic abuse in this way. But for some people an explosive, abusive incident (which may be violent in nature but can include anything that is traumatic) is followed by reconciliation and then a 'honeymoon period' when the abuser behaves kindly. At this stage he may become the perfect husband and father, or he may simply take a break from being as abusive

Cycle of abuse

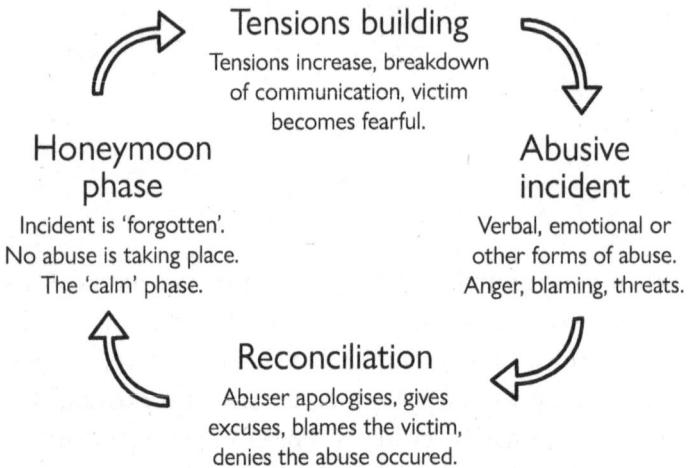

Tensions building
Tensions increase, breakdown
of communication, victim
becomes fearful.

**Honeymoon
phase**
Incident is 'forgotten'.
No abuse is taking place.
The 'calm' phase.

**Abusive
incident**
Verbal, emotional or
other forms of abuse.
Anger, blaming, threats.

Reconciliation
Abuser apologises, gives
excuses, blames the victim,
denies the abuse occured.

as usual. Gradually, this period will give way to a tension-building period. This is the time when we feel as though we are walking on eggshells, where everything we say or do is wrong. After we've experienced this cycle a few times, we start to realise that the explosive incident is on its way.

Some victims of domestic abuse do not experience a honeymoon period – the tension-building period is not episodic but continuous. However, for many of us this honeymoon period and its contrast with the tension-building and violence is confusing. Many survivors describe it as like living with Jekyll and Hyde.

This creates a false sense of hope. We can begin to see the honeymoon version of our partner as 'the real him' and consider the abuse to be out of character. We may make excuses that it's because of stress, or mental health problems, or drink, or drugs. We begin to hope for a time when the honeymoon period will become permanent. It is not unreasonable then for us to have placed our hope in our abusive partners – their behaviour during the honeymoon period gave us reason to do so. But when we can take a step back and see that this behaviour was simply a tactic of abuse, we see that our hope in them was unfounded.

To do

Look again at the hopes you had when you were younger. How do you feel now about your youthful dreams? It may be that the time has passed for you to be able to achieve these dreams, or it may be that you have grown and changed and don't hope for the same things any more. If this is the case, find a way to let go of those dreams and grieve the loss of your unfulfilled hopes. Perhaps you could write them on a piece of paper and safely burn it or bury it somewhere. Or perhaps you could write a poem or paint a picture. It's OK to grieve for the things that never came to pass.

Are there any dreams from your childhood that you still hope for? If so, write them down here and think of one small step you can take on the road to making them a reality.

Section 2: From hopeless to hopeful

For surely I know the plans I have for you, says the
LORD, plans for your welfare and not for harm, to give
you a future with hope.
(Jeremiah 29:11)

How do you feel when you read this verse? Write your
thoughts below.

In section 1 we thought about the false hope we placed in
our abusers, who were never capable of or willing to fulfil
our hopes. When we realise our hopes have been a waste of
time, we can feel hopeless. That unfulfilment can make us
feel as though there's no point in hoping for anything at all,
because it only leads to disappointment. The breakdown of
a relationship we have invested so much of ourselves in can
leave us feeling as if there's no future left for us.

God doesn't see things like that. When we're suffering,
it's common for us to feel angry with God. After all, surely
an omnipotent God can prevent suffering and abuse?
That's something we will dig into in more depth in chapter
3, but for now please know that if you are reading Jeremiah

29:11 and feeling that God has failed to keep a promise, those feelings are normal.

God's promise of hope is not a promise that you will never suffer, nor that times will not be tough. God made this promise to the people of Israel during the Babylonian exile when they were slaves. Jeremiah told the people that their situation would not be changing anytime soon – they would remain in captivity for another seventy years and, during that time, God had a plan for them, a plan to give them a future and a hope. Likewise, when you were experiencing abuse (or if you still are) God had a plan for you that would give you a future and a hope. God still does. You may not be living the life you imagined, but God is with you in your suffering. Unlike fallible humans, God can be relied upon to keep promises and to give us reason to hope.

Rather than giving up on the concept of hope altogether, it's good to consider where we root our hope. Like the Israelites whom Jeremiah was addressing, we may not always feel that we can place our hope in God. God doesn't promise life will always be easy, but does promise to be with us when it's tough. So how do we remain hopeful when God feels far away?

We can find some of the best role models for keeping spiritual hope alive through times of persecution in the Jewish community, a people who have held on to their faith from the time of the earliest human civilisation right up to the present day. They have survived slavery in Egypt, exile in Babylon, Roman occupation and the Holocaust, and still maintain their faith in the face of antisemitism today. How do they do it? They tell stories.

In Exodus 12:26–27, before the exodus had even happened, Moses commanded the people:

'And when your children ask you, "What do you mean by this observance?" you shall say, "It is the passover sacrifice to the LORD, for he passed over the houses of the Israelites in Egypt, when he struck down the Egyptians but spared our houses."' And the people bowed down and worshipped.

Jews have kept the tradition of telling the story of the exodus alive, from the time they were huddled round campfires in the desert, right up to the present day. The story of God's provision and goodness is handed down from one generation to the next, along with the promise and hope that comes with it. Jonathan Sacks, who used to be Chief Rabbi, writes that re-telling the story of the exodus 'gave Jews the most tenacious identity ever held by a nation. In the eras of oppression, it gave hope of freedom. At times of exile, it promised return. It told two hundred generations of Jewish children who they were and of what story they were a part.' He argues that 'we are the stories we tell about ourselves'.[4]

What's your story? Where can you spot signs of hope in your own narrative? As well as reminding ourselves that we can place our hope in God, we can also tell our own stories of strength and valour. What are your stories of

4 J. Sacks, 'Why Storytelling is Essential to Jews and Judaism', 28 January 2020, at: https://www.algemeiner.com/2020/01/28/why-storytelling-is-essential-to-jews-and-judaism/ (accessed 18 December 2024).

survival, strength and capability? You survived abuse, so I know you are tough! Reminding ourselves of our abilities, our strengths and our good God, can give us cause to live our lives filled with real, tangible hope.

To consider

Do you believe that God can be relied on to give you reason to hope? Why or why not?

Can you think of a time in your past when God has been faithful to you?

To do

Try to create a mood board to help you think about your hopes for the future. Take a large piece of paper and find pictures from magazines or from the internet that speak to you. You could paint or draw your vision for your future if you prefer. If you want to use words instead of pictures, you might like to try to create a word cloud. Brainstorm words and phrases that you'd like to associate with your future and add them to the page.

If you don't have a concrete hope yet, that's fine. A mood board or word cloud can help you start to think about the kind of ways you hope to feel in the future.

In her words

I lost many friends due to the abuse. When everything culminated in a crisis, and I had to plead with so-called friends to help, a number of them didn't believe me. Nor did the church that I had attended for nearly thirty years. They didn't even begin to understand or help me to safety. I felt that I was unloved, and unlovable, by them and therefore could not love myself. Over the last four years of recovery, the realisation of how much Jesus loves me has started to change this perception. If he loves me so much that he would die for me – and rescue me from the abuse – couldn't I now love myself?

(Anonymous survivor)

LOVE

2

What happened to me?

Section 1: Pouring from Adam's cup

. . . love is not envious or boastful or arrogant or rude.
It does not insist on its own way; it is not irritable
or resentful; it does not rejoice in wrongdoing, but
rejoices in the truth.
(1 Corinthians 13:4–6)

In chapters 1 and 2 of Genesis we read that both man
and woman were created in God's own image. God
commissioned both man and woman, equally, to steward
and fill the earth. Adam and Eve are shown as equals
who live in harmony, and at the end of chapter 1 this is
described as 'very good'. However, in chapter 3 we read the
story of the Fall. Everything goes wrong and sin enters the
world. As a result, harmony is ruined and there is a power
struggle between Adam and Eve. In verse 16 of the same
chapter, Eve is told, 'Your desire shall be for your husband,
and he shall rule over you.' People's desire to rule, to hold
power over and control one another is a story as old as
time. It is one of the first consequences of sin, and it is the
reason why some people choose to abuse their spouse.

Abuse doesn't happen because of drink or drugs or
mental health problems. It doesn't happen because someone
has anger management issues or because they are stressed. It

doesn't happen because a person is unhappy, misunderstood or had a bad childhood. These things are all excuses made by abusers. Abuse happens because the abuser *chooses* to exert power and control over the other person. Abuse is a choice. It is a sin. It is a sin Adam chose when his first reaction to being found out was to blame Eve. Passing the blame for your mistakes onto your spouse is an abusive behaviour.

The Bible tells us that 'as all die in Adam, so all will be made alive in Christ' (1 Corinthians 15:22). Jesus is often referred to as the second Adam because he puts right what Adam messed up; not only through the cosmic act of salvation that took place on the cross, but also through our everyday lives as we live out Christ's teaching. We can choose to live in sin, or we can choose an alternative way of life – the way that Jesus taught us: love.

In Matthew 22:39–40 Jesus talked about the greatest commandments. He told us to love God and love our neighbour as ourselves. He told us that the entirety of God's law is underpinned by love. In other words, if we want to live the way God desires, we must love. As Christians, we can choose whether we pour into our lives from Jesus' cup (love) or from Adam's cup (sin). Whichever we choose will spill over into our relationships. If my partner and I pour love into our relationship, we will both be loving in our behaviour, and our relationship will be healthy. However, if one of us pours sin into our relationship, unloving and abusive behaviour will result.

The Bible tells us what loving behaviour looks like and, crucially, what it does not look like. We can contrast a loving relationship with an abusive relationship by paraphrasing the famous message about love in Paul's letter to the Corinthians:

> Love is patient, love is kind; abuse is envious, boastful, arrogant and rude. Abuse insists on its own way; it is irritable, resentful and rejoices in wrongdoing. Love rejoices in the truth. Love bears all things, believes all things, hopes all things, endures all things.
> (see 1 Corinthians 13:4–7)

To consider

In the diagram on the next page you will see a model of an abusive relationship, where one person is choosing to pour from Adam's cup into the relationship. Under each of the behaviours listed, try to think of examples of what that might look like in an abusive relationship. There is already one example under each behaviour to get you started.

good idea

Adam's cup
Power and Control

In an unhealthy or abusive relationship one or both people pour from the cup of sin

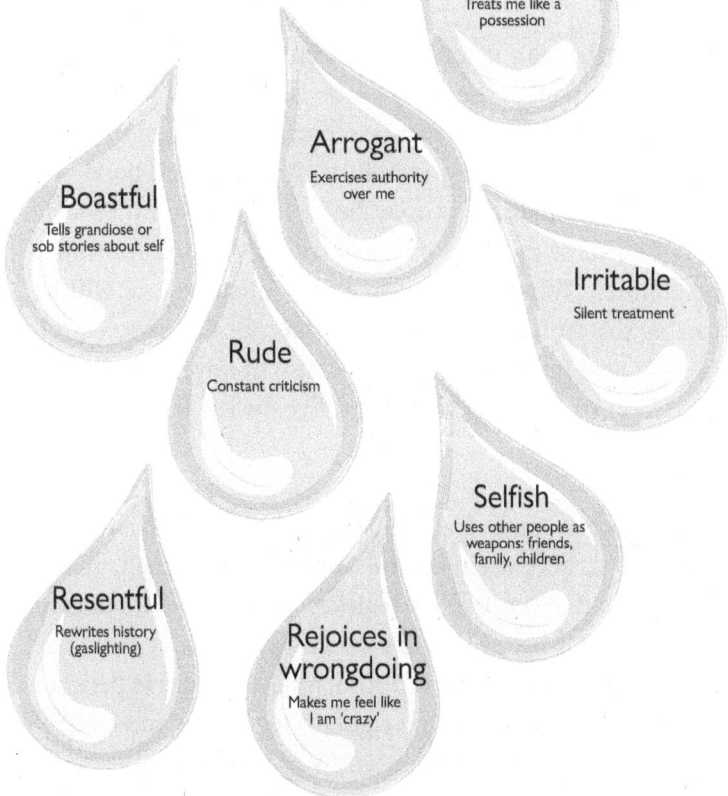

Envy
Treats me like a possession

Arrogant
Exercises authority over me

Boastful
Tells grandiose or sob stories about self

Irritable
Silent treatment

Rude
Constant criticism

Selfish
Uses other people as weapons: friends, family, children

Resentful
Rewrites history (gaslighting)

Rejoices in wrongdoing
Makes me feel like I am 'crazy'

Did you consider the following behaviours?

Envious

Envy arises from a feeling of entitlement and possessiveness. The envious man sees you as a possession and may use jealousy to control you. He may isolate you from other relationships, accuse you of infidelity and attempt to make you feel jealous of other women, by flirting with them or by comparing you with them.

Boastful

The boastful man is interested in curating his own image. In the early days he may 'love bomb' you with gifts, seeking to be seen as Prince Charming. His motivation for any act of kindness is making himself look good. He can be charismatic and may be well liked by others. He may be full of tall tales exaggerating his own importance or abilities. When he fails or makes mistakes, he will be unable to admit he is wrong. If he has not been successful, he may also be full of sob stories. It will never be his fault (just like Adam when he blamed Eve for the Fall).

Arrogant

The arrogant man feels superior to you. This may be because he believes men are superior to women, but it could also be because he believes he is more intelligent than you or is better in some other way. He is likely to use his male privilege to exert authority over you. He believes it is his job, even his divine right, to teach you and control you. The arrogant man infantilises and patronises; he undermines you in front of your children or friends. He undermines your self-confidence.

√ clear

Rude

The man who is rude knows words have power and he uses his words to emotionally abuse you, to tear you down rather than build you up. He may use seemingly innocuous comments to make you feel small, or he may use backhanded compliments or 'banter' as an excuse to insult you. His criticism may become constant, like a dripping tap.

Selfish

The selfish man puts himself first. He will even put himself above his children. He will withhold money from you and may use financial abuse to limit your access to funds and independence. The selfish man will have no qualms about using the children to hurt or control you and may also be sexually abusive, using sex as a weapon and prioritising his own sexual desires.

Irritable

Living with the irritable abuser feels like constantly walking on eggshells. He will use fear to control you. He may use physical abuse, but he may also use intimidation and threats to frighten you. He will seem angry and will fly off the handle easily, but this is a tactic of abuse. When he is with other people, he will probably have no problem keeping his temper.

Resentful

The resentful abuser loves to drag out an argument for as long as possible; no solution will ever make him happy. He may prolong arguments well into the night, not allowing you to sleep. Everything you do will be wrong and he will portray himself as the victim in all circumstances. He will become so skilled at this that you may start to believe you are to blame and he is the victim. He constantly brings up past arguments and he rewrites history, using gaslighting techniques to manipulate your worldview.

Rejoices in wrongdoing

The abusive man knows that he is exerting power and control over you. He revels in it. He may be cruel, but at other times may be lovely. He does this in order to manipulate you. The man rejoicing in his wrongdoing manipulates you so that he can get away with his behaviour for as long as possible. He denies his behaviour, he minimises the abuse and he blames you for it. He works to make you feel as if you are going crazy. He may use other people in order to abuse you, such as friends and family, or his ex.

The (UK) Domestic Abuse Act 2021 says that behaviour is abusive if it consists of

(a) physical or sexual abuse;
(b) violent or threatening behaviour;
(c) controlling or coercive behaviour;
(d) economic abuse;
(e) psychological, emotional or other abuse;
and it does not matter whether the behaviour consists of a single incident or a course of conduct.[5]

---

5   Available to view in full at: https://www.legislation.gov.uk/ukpga/2021/17/section/1/enacted (accessed 9 December 2024).

The abuse we see described in 1 Corinthians 13, which we have expanded on above, fits into all of these categories. Most victims experience just as much, if not more, psychological, emotional and financial abuse as they do physical and sexual. However, the image of domestic abuse in the minds of many is 'beatings'. Often, as survivors we will be asked, 'Did he hit you?'

Many people experience only emotional and psychological abuse, but although society can sometimes be dismissive of this, it is important to know that it can be just as devastating. Emotional abuse *is abuse*. None of us deserve to be abused in any way. It is a sin and, as we can see from reading 1 Corinthians 13, it is the opposite of love.

To do

Because you have been thinking about the abuse you experienced, spend some time now gently taking care of yourself by doing something that makes you feel happy. You did not deserve to be treated that way. You are a daughter of God, and you deserve to be loved. Start with loving yourself. What could you do for yourself that makes you feel loved? Maybe it's cooking yourself some good food, or giving yourself five minutes to sit down with a brew and a book. Maybe you could buy yourself flowers. Write below what you commit to do for yourself.

Section 2: Pouring from Jesus' cup

'I came that they may have life, and have it abundantly.'
(John 10:10)

As we've discussed, the abusive behaviours described in the Bible as the antithesis of love fall into these categories: financial, physical, emotional/psychological and sexual abuse. These kinds of abuse are equally damaging to us. When abuse happens to a person of faith there is usually also an element of spiritual abuse within the experience. This can be difficult for us to talk about with secular support agencies that do not share our faith.

In abusive Christian relationships, spiritual abuse trickles down into every other form of abuse. This adds another dimension to the trauma we experience. Consider each of the abusive behaviours again and think about how they might look specifically for a Christian. I've started you off with an example for each, but add your own thoughts underneath.

Envious

He may tell you that Eve was made *for* Adam, that your purpose is to belong to him. He may insist on 'the Billy Graham rule' that says men and women should never be alone together, to prevent you from having friendships with other men. He may compare you with other women at church and tell you they are better Christian wives.

Boastful

He may claim special spiritual giftings or authority. He may tell you that God has told him he is to marry you. This may make you feel that rejecting him is rejecting God's will. He may seek out positions of power within the church and may appear to be a 'pillar of the community'.

Arrogant

He may use his male privilege to insist that you submit to him or to enforce gender roles. He may use verses from the Bible to insist that men are superior to women.

Rude

He may tell you that you are a disappointment to God, that you've let God down, that you are a bad Christian. He may call you a 'Jezebel' and may make you feel that your sexual desires are sinful.

Selfish

He may make you feel that you are obligated to do certain things, such as give up your job to look after the home, or have sex with him on demand. He may use the concept of service and humility to convince you to run around after him and always put him first.

Irritable

He may appeal to religious ideas about gender differences to convince you that he is unable to control his temper. He may say that his bad temperedness or even violence is because of his created masculinity. He may make threats to ostracise you from your church family or ruin your reputation within the church. He may threaten you with hell.

Resentful

The resentful abuser rewrites history to manipulate your worldview, and in the same way he may put a spin on sermons or Bible passages to manipulate your faith view. You will not be able to deviate from or disagree with his doctrinal position.

Rejoices in wrongdoing

He will use your faith to keep you in the relationship by telling you that God hates divorce. He may play the victim in church and convince people that you are the abusive one or that you are crazy. He may do this by asking people to pray for you, thus making himself look like a kind and thoughtful husband.

Sadly, spiritual abuse doesn't just happen at home; it can happen in the Church as well. Sometimes this is through a misuse of power and a sinful need for control, but also, unintentionally, it can be due to a poor understanding of theology, through naivety or because of the culture. When spiritually abusive behaviours are present in church, they will galvanise abusive men and compound our experience at home.

In 2018, Christian blogger Sarah Bessey asked women on Twitter to share things that only Christian women hear. Here are some of the examples of the heart-breaking, real-life things women said they had been told:

'You are an amazing leader! You'd make an excellent pastor's wife someday!' (Sarah Bessey)

'Keep waiting and God will bring your Boaz to you.' (Joy Beth Smith)

'Biblical womanhood can be defined by marriage and motherhood.' (Joy Beth Smith)

'Stop being so aggressive. You should wait to be "found".' (Cici Adams)

'Girl, don't buy a house! How is your husband supposed to feel like a man if he doesn't buy your first one?' (Tia J. Davis)

'Your clothes can cause boys to sin.' (Amber Wingfield)
'You speak five languages and have a doctoral degree?
    Children's ministry is your calling!' (Sara Eggers)
'You're too strong, honey. You've got to let him lead if you
    want a man.' (Jill Marie Richardson)
'Dress modestly because men are too weak. Also, men are
    in charge of you because they are spiritually superior.'
    (Stephanie Long)
'Maybe people will listen to you if you stop sounding so
    angry.' (Sarah Beth Caplin)[6]

Add your own examples to this list. It could be things your abuser said to you, or it could be things you have heard in church that you don't think you would have heard if you had been a man. They don't necessarily have to be rude, unkind or abusive. They can be seemingly innocuous things – like, for example, the question my pastor asked me when I told him I was thinking of going back to work when my children started school: 'Have you got your husband's permission?'

6 Available at: https://www.cbeinternational.org/resource/55-things-only-christian-women-hear/ (accessed 19 November 2024).

To consider

Jesus said in John 10:10, 'I came that they may have life and have it abundantly.' Jesus came to give us life here and now, not just in eternity, not just any life, but an abundant life. Write down everything you think of when you hear the phrase 'abundance of life'.

Now look at the two lists. Compare your understanding of abundant life to the list of Christian women's experiences above. Do they seem in any way similar, or even compatible?

God wants our lives to be wonderful, to be fulfilled abundantly. Any ideas that teach us we are worth less than men, that we are subordinate, that we should not be able to use our strengths, talents and abilities, and that we should be satisfied with less, are not from God.

To do

Throughout this chapter we have looked at what love is not. Jesus offers us an alternative. Christians can choose to live as redeemed people, pouring from Jesus' cup. On the next page is a diagram that uses the 'love is' statements from 1 Corinthians 13 to show what a healthy, loving relationship looks like. Look at the model and read the examples under each behaviour. Use this to think about what matters most to you in a relationship. There's space at the end of the chapter for you to list the most important behaviours you would expect to see in a relationship. Remember, we are not talking about a perfect person here, simply a decent human who loves their partner.

In a healthy
relationship both
people pour love
into the relationship

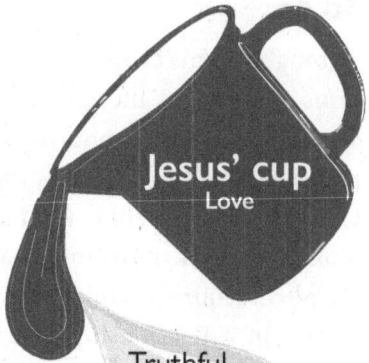

Jesus' cup
Love

Patient
Able to resolve conflict
in ways that make
both of us happy
**Demonstrates tolerance
and gentleness even
when frustrated**
Loves me 'warts 'n' all'

Truthful
Is honest
Is faithful
Recognises that truth
brings freedom and
blossoming and so
does not weaponise
opinions as truth but
seeks to encourage

Kind
Treats me as they'd
like me to treat
them
**Treats me and
others with
respect**
Seeks to serve
me and others

Trust
**Encourages
my friendships**
Sees the
best in me
Is trustworthy
Is accountable
for own
behaviour

Hopeful
Believes in me
**Supports my
dreams**
Wants us to
build a future
together
**Is a good role
model**

Never Ends
Is stable and consistent
Has firm boundaries
and respects mine
Goalposts do not move
Love is neverwithdrawn
as a punishment

Protects
Shares my burdens
I feel safe to express
myself
**Is a comfort and
help in tough times**
Will ask for help
when needed

Perseveres
Pulls together with
me/does their fair share
**Treats me as an equal
in all matters**
Values my opinion
**Remains positive
when life gets hard**

Patient

A patient partner knows your flaws and still loves you. There is no expectation on you to be perfect. He is tolerant and gentle even when he is feeling frustrated and when there is conflict in the relationship. He will look to find a resolution that is mutually beneficial for both of you. He can navigate conflict without being aggressive.

Kind

A kind partner treats you in the way he wants to be treated. He is respectful and generous, and he seeks to serve, putting your needs above his own.

Truthful

The truthful person is honest and faithful. So your partner does not keep secrets or commit adultery. He does not insult you or hurt you under the guise of 'speaking the truth in love'. He recognises that the truth causes people to blossom and as such seeks to encourage you.

Protective

The wording of 'bears all things' in the original Greek that the Bible was written in carries implications of bearing up under pressure. A loving spouse seeks to be a safe shelter during a storm. He shares your burdens and provides comfort in difficult times. With him you feel safe to express yourself and be vulnerable. He also recognises that this is an equal partnership and will ask for help when he needs it.

Trusting and trustworthy

He believes the best of you and encourages your friendships and other relationships. He gets on well with your friends and family, and is secure in your relationship. He is also trustworthy and reliable; he takes responsibility and is accountable for his own behaviour. He will apologise, and mean it, when he is wrong.

Hopeful

He genuinely wants you to build a future together and work towards doing that, being a good father and/or role model if you have children. He contributes not only financially but also in terms of housework. He believes in you and your abilities. He encourages and supports you to pursue the things that are important to you. You feel hopeful about your future when you are around him.

Persevering

The Bible says that it's important a couple are 'equally yoked' so that they can persevere together. If two oxen pull a cart, they need to be equal in strength, or the cart will be pulled unevenly and will break. A partner who perseveres sees you as an equal in every way. He will ask for and value your opinion and you will make decisions together. You pull in the same direction. He will remain positive and committed even when it is difficult.

Never ending

The love a consistent partner shows is stable and predictable. He is not fickle in his love and would never withhold love as some kind of punishment. His love underpins his attitude even when he is unhappy with you. He has firm boundaries and you know where you stand with him – the goalposts do not move. He respects your boundaries.

What happened to me?

The most important behaviours I would expect to see in a relationship are . . .

In her words

It has been an incredibly tumultuous and soul-destroying two years of post-separation abuse that ramped up since leaving an almost fourteen-year 'godly' marriage. It was anything but godly and something I have had to deconstruct in almost every aspect of myself – my beliefs, my faith, my marriage and my children – and start again. It will always be a scar in our story, and we are still navigating the varied abuse tactics since the separation.

I know that I need to use my voice to speak up and help raise awareness of what domestic abuse and coercive control really looks like and feels like, particularly in supposed 'Christian' relationships.

I want to challenge the many myths, stereotypes and misogynistic attitudes that lock victims in those situations. I want to speak up for my children's sakes, my sake, and every other man, woman and child who may not be able to say, 'No, this is not acceptable; this is not my fault, and the only person who is responsible is the abuser.'

More importantly, I want people to know they are free to leave and not feel shame, guilt or condemnation from church leaders or other misguided people. Divorce is not disobeying God or the Church. Jesus came to bring freedom to the captives and heal the broken, regardless of someone's marital status.
(Anonymous survivor)

3

Why did this happen?

Section 1: The world's beliefs

Do not be conformed to this world, but be transformed
by the renewing of your minds.
(Romans 12:2)

When abuse takes place, we may think that the abuser
is out of control. He may make excuses such as: 'I was
drunk'; 'I didn't know what I was doing'; 'I blacked out';
'The red mist came down'; 'You pushed my buttons and I
just lost it.' We know these excuses aren't valid, because
most abusive people manage to control themselves in
other situations. They don't behave abusively towards
their boss, and they don't behave abusively towards us in
front of others. In most cases, if your minister knocked on
your door in the middle of your abuser's rage, he would
immediately calm down. Why? Because he is in full
control. Abuse is always a choice. As adults we know the
difference between right and wrong, and if we use abuse,
we are making a choice to exert power over another person
to control them.

This desire to control is driven by a sense of entitlement.
A belief that the abuser should be dominant and we should
be subservient. This is why abuse is often gender based –
many perpetrators still hold the belief that 'a real man'

36

takes control of 'his woman' and that a 'good woman' will obey her man.

Our society still subtly creates expectations about how men should behave, from songs like 'Stand by Your Man' to fairytale princess stories where the meek helpless woman is saved by Prince Charming. Most CEOs and politicians are men, while 70% of household chores are still carried out by women, even in households where both adults work. Women still take on their husband's surname after being 'given away' by their fathers. For the majority of adults alive today, it was only in their lifetime that it became illegal for a man to rape his wife.[7] These cultural influences mean that many of us, while we may not realise it, will hold some underlying beliefs about the roles of men and women, and for some people these beliefs can lead to abusive behaviour.

Some abusive people may appear to be egalitarian in nature – they may even claim to be feminists. If asked, they would say, 'Of course I don't believe that men should dominate women.' Human beings are complicated. Our beliefs are often so deep rooted we may not even realise we hold them. We may even hold two sets of contradictory beliefs at the same time. Psychologists call this cognitive dissonance.

Nelson Mandela gave a personal example of this phenomenon in his book *The Long Walk to Freedom*. He explained that as he was leaving Robben Island, where he had been imprisoned for fighting against apartheid, he noticed the pilot was black and momentarily had to

---

7 In most Western countries the law made marital rape illegal during the 1980s or 1990s: UK 1992, USA 1993, Australia state by state between 1981 and 1995, Canada 1983. In many countries marital rape is still legal.

quell his panic, as he wondered how a black man could fly a plane.[8] Even though he *knew* that black people were no less capable than white people, he had unintentionally absorbed some of the beliefs of the culture he was raised in. As a result, he had a deep-rooted faulty belief that he had to work to challenge.

Nelson Mandela recognised the untrue thought pattern, but most of us only recognise that we have absorbed faulty beliefs when they have a negative impact on our lives. Perpetrators of abuse benefit from their beliefs. They hold the power and the control, and therefore rarely recognise that there is a problem.

In addition, recognising and admitting cognitive dissonance is uncomfortable. Nobody likes to admit they are wrong. Therefore, many of us attempt to justify or explain away our behaviour. It is far more common for a perpetrator of abuse to minimise their behaviour, blame the victim for it, or even flat out deny it, than it is for them to recognise their sense of entitlement. The longer they exist within a society that subtly reinforces stereotypes about men and women, the more deep rooted those beliefs become.

What beliefs do you think perpetrators of domestic abuse may hold about men and women?

---

8 Nelson Mandela, *The Long Walk to Freedom* (London: Abacus, 1995).

Perhaps you've written down the belief that men are superior to women, or that women need a man to protect them and control them. Perhaps you've mentioned the idea that men are more rational and women are more emotional, or the belief that raising children and working in the home is women's work. Perhaps you've noted the idea that women should not deny their husbands sex, that men deserve a wife, that women are men's property or that men are not able to control their violent and sexual tendencies and should not be held accountable for their behaviour.

Consider each of the following aspects of secular culture and see if you can think of one or two examples of these beliefs being played out.

- Media and advertising

- Music

- Literature

- Film and TV

- Toys and education

• Politics and history

• Culture and ritual

Perhaps you wrote down adverts for cleaning products showing men incapable of cleaning the house, or songs such as Dolly Parton's 'Jolene' or Aerosmith's 'Used to Love Her'. Did you consider fairytales, or characters such as *Hamlet*'s Ophelia or Miss Havisham from *Great Expectations*? Both went mad because they didn't have a man to take care of them. Did you note how women in action films often ask, 'What should we do now?' before falling into the hero's arms at the end? Did you consider the toys we give girls and boys to play with, or expectations we have of girls and boys in the classroom? Did you think about how long it took women to get the vote? Or that women used to be locked in asylums for being teenage mothers or having post-natal depression? Perhaps you considered the witch trials of the seventeenth century. Or maybe you considered lad culture. Or the way media coverage of abuse and rape often questions the integrity of the victim.

To consider

There is much within secular culture that feeds and embeds sexist and abusive beliefs, but it's not just men who absorb these ideas. If we have internalised the misogynistic beliefs our culture teaches us, it can make it easier for abusive attitudes and eventually abusive behaviour to become normalised. Most of us don't consider ourselves to be holding sexist beliefs. Ask yourself the following questions to help you consider whether you may also have picked up some unhealthy notions about men and women. Have you ever . . .

- referred to a man as 'under the thumb', 'henpecked' or 'whipped'?
- made jokes about men being unable to do housework or change nappies, or needing to be housetrained?
- felt obligated to have sex when you didn't want to?
- apologised for your partner's behaviour?
- felt guilty about your partner's behaviour?
- deferred to male authority?
- judged another woman on her sexual behaviour in a way you wouldn't judge a man?
- felt disappointed or worried that the assistant in the DIY shop/garage/hospital was a woman?
- worried about leaving your child with a male nursery nurse?
- called a female boss a 'bitch' or a 'ballbreaker' or 'hard-faced', or said she slept her way to the top?
- apologised for nagging or counselled other women not to nag?
- downplayed your humour or intelligence?

If you've done any of these things you might have taken on some of those untrue beliefs about men and women. It's difficult to challenge abuse in a society that denies it, minimises it or blames us for it. Can you think of anything else you may have said or done because of subconscious beliefs about gender roles?

To do

As you go about your daily life in the next couple of days, look out for occurrences of 'everyday sexism'. These feed abusive beliefs about men and women. You could make a note of them in the blank space below. If you are feeling creative, you might want to buy a newspaper or some magazines and see if you can make a collage of messages you receive from the media about what it means to be a woman. If you are stuck, take a look at the website everydaysexism.com, where women from around the world document their experiences and anecdotes about everyday sexism.

Section 2: The Church's beliefs

He heals the broken-hearted, and binds up their
wounds.
(Psalm 147:3)

Given that it's secular culture that feeds unhelpful beliefs,
surely we shouldn't be seeing abuse happen in Christian
culture. We're supposed to be different from the rest of the
world, right? You'd think so, wouldn't you?

Several bodies of research have found that domestic
abuse happens within Christian relationships at a similar
rate to the rest of the world. In fact, the only factor that
affects how likely you are to experience domestic abuse
is gender: between April 2019 and March 2020, 77% of
victims in domestic abuse prosecutions in the UK were
female, while 92% of defendants were male.[9]

Religion, wealth, education and race do not have any
effect on how likely a person is to become a victim or
a perpetrator of domestic abuse. Within the worldwide
population, one in three women[10] will experience domestic
abuse at some point in her lifetime. In the US, Canada,
Australia, UK and across Europe, the figure stands at one
in four women.

In 2002 the UK Methodist Church carried out surveys

---

9 ONS, 'Domestic abuse in England and Wales overview: November 2020':
https://www.ons.gov.uk/peoplepopulationandcommunity/crimeandjustice/
bulletins/domesticabuseinenglandandwalesoverview/november2020 (accessed 21
November 2024).

10 World Health Organization, 'Violence against women': http://www.who.int/
mediacentre/factsheets/fs239/en/ (accessed 21 November 2024).

with ministers and lay workers into the prevalence of domestic abuse within the church. They found that one in four women and one in nine men reported experiencing domestic abuse from a partner as an adult.[11] In 2012 the Evangelical Alliance's 'How's the family?' research found that 10% of respondents in churches within the Evangelical Alliance said they had been the victim of physical abuse at least once.[12] Then in 2018 Coventry University and the University of Leicester carried out surveys across denominations in Cumbria and found that one in four churchgoers reported experiencing abusive behaviours within their *current* relationship.[13]

This isn't limited to the UK church. In 2021 the National Anglican Family Violence Research Report, published by Australian researchers from Charles Sturt University, found that 22% of Anglicans answered 'yes' when asked, 'Have you been in a violent relationship with any partner?' In comparison, they found 15% of the general population answered 'yes' to this question.[14] While worldwide studies on the prevalence of domestic abuse within Christian households are scant, all available evidence demonstrates that the Christian faith is not the protective factor against domestic abuse that Christians would expect it to be.

11 'Domestic violence and the Methodist Church', at: https://www.methodist.org.uk/downloads/conf-domestic-violence-the-way-forward-2002.pdf (accessed 21 November 2024).

12 Available at: https://www.eauk.org/church/resources/snapshot/upload/EA-FAMILY-REPORT-WEB.pdf (accessed 21 November 2024).

13 'In Churches Too: key findings', at: https://www.restored-uk.org/about/our-research/ (accessed 21 November 2024).

14 'Domestic abuse more prevalent among Anglican churchgoers, new report finds', at: https://amp.abc.net.au/article/100204552 (accessed 21 November 2024).

Most cultures and sub-cultures across the world have elements that can feed into the underlying belief that men should dominate women, and Christianity is no different. When a perpetrator is a Christian, he will find aspects of Christian culture, whatever country he lives in or denomination he belongs to, that support his beliefs. He will even interpret Scripture in ways that suggest his beliefs are unquestioningly biblical. Christian victims of domestic abuse may feel additional pressure not only to be 'good women', but to be 'good Christian women'. Christian perpetrators of abuse may well believe themselves to be the God-appointed head of the household with a spiritual responsibility to exercise control over their wives.

Let me tell you about my friend Anne.[15] Anne was a young woman from church who used to babysit for me. Older women with families were encouraged to mentor younger women. Younger women in turn were encouraged to babysit and spend time with families in preparation for their future. There was an assumption that every young Christian woman would become a wife and mother. I felt a responsibility towards Anne.

One day she talked to me about trying to maintain friendships with the young men in the church in a wholesome way. She told me she just hadn't realised how 'visual' men were. Apparently one of the young men in church had told her that when young women carried their bags with the strap across the body so that it sat between

---

15 Not her real name.

and separated the breasts, he found it sexy. Anne said that this revelation was eye-opening for her, as previously she'd just been carrying her bag in a way that was comfortable. Now she was careful not to let the bag strap sit between her breasts, because she didn't want to tempt her brothers in Christ. I applauded Anne for her commitment to purity and for being thoughtful towards the men in her life.

Now, when I look back, I wish I'd told Anne that she shouldn't have to go through life worrying about something as innocuous as the way she carries her bag. I wish I'd said that if a man cannot control himself around her just because he can see the outline of her breasts, this is his issue – not hers. I wish I'd told her that she's responsible for her own behaviour, not the behaviour of the men in her life. I also wish I'd asked her how her friend's comments had made her feel and told her that it was not appropriate for him to be making comments about her body.

It is not always specific biblical teachings that feed into abusive beliefs, but rather cultural ideas, practices and emphases. The assumption that every young woman will become a wife and mother encourages the belief that women's lives revolve around men. The emphasis on purity can make girls believe their worth is tied to their sexual choices. And, of course, teaching girls to take responsibility for boys' sexual behaviour makes it much easier for perpetrators of abuse to minimise that abuse and blame their victims. Across Christian denominations and nations, these cultural aspects may differ, but the effects will be the same.

Take a look at the beliefs abusive men may hold that you wrote down in section 1 on page 36. In the space below, consider what aspects of Christian culture, teaching and doctrine may feed into those beliefs. For now, you don't need to consider whether those aspects of our faith are right or wrong. Simply consider what may feed abusive behaviours.

Perhaps you considered biblical figures who are portrayed as temptresses, such as Eve or Delilah or Jezebel. Maybe you've heard the proverb that says it's better to sleep on the roof than in the house with a nagging wife (Proverbs 21:9). Maybe you considered how our modern-day marriage ceremony, where the groom asks permission to propose and then the father of the bride 'gives her away', is based on the Old Testament where wives and daughters were considered property. Maybe you considered passages from the Bible that seem to say that women are the 'weaker sex' (1 Peter 3:7) or that wives should submit (Ephesians 5:22) and that God hates divorce (Malachi 2:16). Perhaps you even considered that there is no clear biblical instruction that allows a woman to divorce specifically because of abuse. Or perhaps you thought about famous pastors, such as John Piper, who have said that a woman may have to endure abuse 'for a season'.[16] You may have written about the importance of forgiveness and the emphasis on two-parent families within the Church.

There is much within church teaching and culture that emboldens abusers. Abusers can, and will, use this to control us, belittle us and keep us trapped in the relationship. This can leave us feeling confused as to which things are really God's instructions for us and what is simply man's misinterpretation. For Christian women, working out which of our beliefs are fruitful and bring us fullness of life, and which are unhealthy and unhelpful, is as much a part of recovery as working through the trauma of being abused.

This can be doubly challenging if our church has discouraged questioning. It is OK to ask questions. In fact, the Bible tells us, 'Do not believe every spirit, but test the spirits to see whether they are from God; for many false prophets have gone out into the world' (1 John 4:1). Testing the things human beings have taught us about God is not the same as testing God. Asking questions is good and part of the process of spiritual discernment. It should be encouraged. Do not be afraid to question aspects of Christian culture that may have made it easier for someone to abuse you.

---

16 During a sermon Q&A Piper was asked, 'What should a wife's submission to her husband look like when her husband is abusive?' Part of his answer was, 'If it's not requiring her to sin, but simply hurting her, then I think she endures verbal abuse for a season; she endures perhaps being smacked one night.' See John Piper, 'Does a woman submit to abuse?' available at: https://www.youtube.com/watch?v=3OkUPc2NLrM (accessed 9 December 2024).

To consider

We can start the process of understanding how our faith was used to abuse us by considering the following questions:

What did I believe that made it easier to belittle me?

What did I believe that made it easier to control me?

What did I believe that made me stay?

To do

If you feel able to when you pray over the next week or so, take to God those beliefs you've just written. It doesn't matter whether you still hold those beliefs or not. Just put them out there while you're talking to God.

In her words

Outside the city wall

He meets me outside the city wall.
He too was an outcast.
He comes into the barren landscape.
I look into his eyes and see my pain.
He was broken.
He was bruised.
He was despised.
Outside the city wall he was crucified.

He holds out his hands to me.
I am not alone.
It is barren.
It is desolate.
The church is clapping and singing.
The one who I thought loved me is there with them, welcomed,
While I am outside.
They are blinded, they do not see, they do not understand.
But he sees, he knows.

Sunday morning,
He walks away from the city and comes to me outside
the city wall.
He puts his hand on my heart,
The hand that bears the marks of the nails.

He looks into my eyes,
I know, I know, I know.
I am here, I am here, I am here.
You are not alone.
(Caroline, 2019)

Bible study 1

Love and the law

When the Pharisees heard that he had silenced the Sadducees, they gathered together, and one of them, a lawyer, asked him a question to test him. 'Teacher, which commandment in the law is the greatest?' He said to him, '"You shall love the Lord your God with all your heart, and with all your soul, and with all your mind." This is the greatest and first commandment. And a second is like it: "You shall love your neighbour as yourself." On these two commandments hang all the law and the prophets.'
(Matthew 22:34–40)

The religious leaders of Jesus' time were fed up with him. He'd preached that their obedience of the law did not go far enough. They prided themselves on not being murderers and adulterers, while harbouring anger and lust in their hearts. Jesus said that people had to be better than the religious leaders, whom he called 'hypocrites', 'whitewashed tombs' and 'sons of snakes'. No wonder they didn't like him.

Jesus antagonised them further by breaking their rules. He worked on the Sabbath, gleaning in the fields and healing people. He allowed his disciples to eat without following ritual washing procedures. He touched the unclean and didn't care. And he was accused of not paying his temple tax and of blaspheming. Determined to silence him, both the Pharisees and the Sadducees posed a series of tricky theological questions, but he always had an answer for them. Eventually, the Pharisees cornered him with the question, 'Which is the greatest commandment?' He had previously accused them of not following the law properly, while, from their perspective, his own attitude to the strict rules of religion was blasé. So they approached him, demanding he explain how he discerned God's law.

Rather than being blasé about the rules, Jesus was putting human well-being over the law, showing us where his priorities lay. God's law was not designed to enslave us in situations that cause us harm. Rather it was designed for our communal well-being. Jesus recognised that there may be times when following the letter of the law, without understanding the spirit of it, would not be the most loving way to behave. For example, the letter of the law says that we should not work on the Sabbath, but a doctor may *need* to work on the Sabbath to save a person's life. While taking a break once a week is generally a good rule that brings about our communal well-being, this is an example that shows it does not always work. An individual may have to break the rule, despite it being generally helpful, in order to do the loving and morally right thing. Jesus recognised that what is right and wrong is not always black and white. He knew that rules and laws can be unhelpful if they are considered unbreachable rather than taken as a general guideline.

When Jesus was asked how we go about discerning right from wrong – in other words, how we live with those shades of grey – Jesus gave us the commandment to love, first and foremost. He said that all the other rules are rooted in love. The Pharisees had it the wrong way round. They followed the letter of the law, but they did not understand that the spirit of the law was love. Worse, they imposed the letter of the law in unloving and harmful ways.

To consider

Reflect on the following questions and write your thoughts under each one.

When Jesus said, 'On these two commandments hang all the law and the prophets', what did he mean?

Did Jesus mean that the rest of the 'rules' were redundant?

How can we apply 'the law' to our lives with love?

If love means keeping the spirit rather than the letter of the law, might we sometimes have to break a rule in order to fulfil the law of love?

What might this mean for the law around marriage and divorce?

To do

Read the passage below from 1 John:

> God abides in those who confess that Jesus is the Son of God, and they abide in God. So we have known and believe the love that God has for us. God is love, and those who abide in love abide in God, and God abides in them. Love has been perfected among us in this: that we may have boldness on the day of judgement, because as he is, so are we in this world. There is no fear in love, but perfect love casts out fear; for fear has to do with punishment, and whoever fears has not reached perfection in love. We love because he first loved us. Those who say, 'I love God', and hate their brothers or sisters, are liars; for those who do not love a brother or sister whom they have seen, cannot love God whom they have not seen. The commandment we have from him is this: those who love God must love their brothers and sisters also.
> (1 John 4:15–21)

Jesus told us to love, first and foremost, but it's important to understand what love actually looks like. John describes love as the essence of God. As Jesus is God incarnate, we can understand what love is by looking to the example of Jesus.

John also tells us that we can discern whether or not somebody really knows God by looking at their version of love. Notably, if their version of love causes us to live in fear, or if it resembles hatred more than it resembles Jesus, then it is not love and it is not from God.

Have a think about the following questions.

Does anything stand out to you from 1 John 4:15–21 about what love does and does not look like?

What does this say about the 'love' we experience when we are in an abusive relationship?

We read in 1 John 4:16 that God *is* love, and 1 Corinthians 13 gives us a description of what love looks like, so what does this tell us about the character of God and how God relates to us?

In her words

The biggest lesson I learned from this experience is radical honesty and authenticity. I fell in love with the idea of someone. I lived with an image that wasn't real. I was pressured to live the perfect middle-class life while being poorly treated. It made me construct a false reality. Since I left, and have been trying to rebuild my life, God's continually taught me to rely daily on him and his Spirit. The fact that he desires truth in the inner person is freeing, as it makes us free to be ourselves.

(Anonymous survivor)

My notes

My notes

4

Where is God in all this?

Section 1: Does God care that I was abused?

You have kept count of my tossings; put my tears in your bottle. Are they not in your record?
(Psalm 56:8)

Domestic abuse can have a profound effect on our faith and on our relationship with God. It is natural to wonder where God is in abusive situations. Some people may question their belief in God. Some people may feel angry with or let down by God. Some people may feel that it's their own fault; that they weren't a good enough Christian or didn't have enough faith. Others won't know what to feel. Most will feel confused and have a lot of questions. This is OK. All of our feelings are valid. God has big enough shoulders to handle our hurt, our disappointment and our rage.

The Psalms contain the whole breadth of human emotion. There are times when the psalmist praises God with all his heart, yet at other times he rails at God. There are times when he feels loved, and times when he feels that God is far away. The psalmist wrestles with anger and often prays for revenge. He is human. This humanity is included in the Bible to let us know it's normal, and to remind us that God cares so deeply for us, even when it doesn't feel that way.

Read Psalm 56:

Be gracious to me, O God, for people trample on me;
    all day long foes oppress me;
my enemies trample on me all day long,
    for many fight against me.
O Most High, when I am afraid,
    I put my trust in you.
In God, whose word I praise,
    in God I trust; I am not afraid;
    what can flesh do to me?
All day long they seek to injure my cause;
    all their thoughts are against me for evil.
They stir up strife, they lurk,
    they watch my steps.
As they hoped to have my life,
so repay them for their crime; in wrath cast down
    the peoples, O God!
You have kept count of my tossings;
    put my tears in your bottle.
    Are they not in your record?
Then my enemies will retreat
    on the day when I call.
    This I know, that God is for me.
In God, whose word I praise,
    in the LORD, whose word I praise,
    in God I trust; I am not afraid.
    What can a mere mortal do to me?

My vows to you I must perform, O God;
  I will render thank-offerings to you.
For you have delivered my soul from death,
  and my feet from falling,
so that I may walk before God
  in the light of life.

To consider

Does this psalm resonate with you? If so, how?

Whose side does it say God is on – the victim's or the abuser's?

How does God react to abuse?

If God is on your side and weeps when you are abused, how is God likely to feel when you escape abuse?

How do you feel about the notion that God keeps your tears in a jar?

Some people feel comforted by this; others feel angry at the thought of God weeping alongside them and collecting their tears in a jar. It's reasonable to feel that an omnipotent God could do something other than empathise. One of the things that can challenge our faith is when our prayers for our abuser to change seem to go unanswered. The Bible is full of examples of violent, murderous men whom God changed and redeemed. It can be devastating to feel that this isn't happening to the violent men in our lives.

Here are two examples of those biblical stories. One is David's story from the Old Testament, and the other is the story of Saul/Paul from the New Testament.

David

And the LORD sent Nathan to David. He came to him and said to him, 'There were two men in a certain city, one rich and the other poor. The rich man had very many flocks and herds; but the poor man had nothing but one little ewe lamb, which he had bought. He brought it up, and it grew up with him and with his children; it used to eat of his meagre fare and drink from his cup, and lie in his bosom, and it was like a daughter to him. Now there came a traveller to the rich man, and he was loath to take one of his own flock or herd to prepare for the wayfarer who had come to him, but he took the poor man's lamb and prepared that for the guest who had come to him.' Then David's anger was greatly kindled against the man. He said to Nathan, 'As the LORD lives, the man who has done this deserves to die; he shall restore the lamb fourfold, because he did this thing and because he had no pity.'

Nathan said to David, 'You are the man! Thus says the LORD, the God of Israel: I anointed you king over Israel, and I rescued you from the hand of Saul; I gave you your master's house, and your master's wives into your bosom, and gave you the house of Israel and of Judah; and if that had been too little, I would have added as much more. Why have you despised the word of the LORD, to do what is evil in his sight? You have struck down Uriah the Hittite with the sword, and have taken his wife to be your wife, and have killed him with the sword of the Ammonites. Now therefore the sword shall never depart from your house, for you have despised me, and have taken the wife of Uriah the Hittite to be your wife. Thus says the LORD: I will raise up trouble against you from within your own house, and I will take your wives before your eyes, and give them to your neighbour, and he shall lie with your wives in the sight of this very sun. For you did it secretly; but I will do this thing before all Israel, and before the sun.' David said to Nathan, 'I have sinned against the LORD.' Nathan said to David, 'Now the LORD has put away your sin; you shall not die.'

(2 Samuel 12:1–13)

Saul/Paul

Meanwhile Saul, still breathing threats and murder against the disciples of the Lord, went to the high priest and asked him for letters to the synagogues at Damascus, so that if he found any who belonged to the Way, men or women, he might bring them bound to Jerusalem. Now as he was going along and approaching Damascus, suddenly a light from heaven flashed around him. He fell to the ground and heard a voice saying to him, 'Saul, Saul, why do you persecute me?' He asked, 'Who are you, Lord?' The reply came, 'I am Jesus, whom you are persecuting. But get up and enter the city, and you will be told what you are to do.' The men who were travelling with him stood speechless because they heard the voice but saw no one. Saul got up from the ground, and though his eyes were open, he could see nothing; so they led him by the hand and brought him into Damascus. For three days he was without sight and neither ate nor drank.

Now there was a disciple in Damascus named Ananias. The Lord said to him in a vision, 'Ananias.' He answered, 'Here I am, Lord.' The Lord said to him, 'Get up and go to the street called Straight, and at the house of Judas look for a man of Tarsus named Saul. At this moment he is praying, and he has seen in a vision a man named Ananias come in and lay his hands on him so that he might regain his sight.' But Ananias answered, 'Lord, I have heard from many about this man, how much evil he has done to your saints in Jerusalem, and here he has authority from the chief priests to bind all who invoke your name.' But the Lord said to him, 'Go, for he is an instrument whom I have chosen to bring my name before Gentiles and kings and before the people of Israel; I myself will show him how much he must suffer for the sake of my name.' So Ananias went and entered the house. He laid his hands on Saul and said, 'Brother Saul, the Lord Jesus, who appeared to you on your way here, has sent me so that you may regain your sight and be filled with the Holy Spirit.' And immediately something like scales fell from his eyes, and his sight was restored. Then he got up and was baptized, and after taking some food, he regained his strength. (Acts 9:1–19)

In these stories, both David and Saul recognised their sin. They both repented and chose to change. There are other stories in the Bible of men who chose *not* to repent and change, such as Pharaoh who would not repent of enslaving the Israelites, and the rich young ruler who left disappointed because he felt he couldn't manage the sacrifice involved in the call to repentance.

Throughout the Bible we see that God does change sinners, often dramatically, but only if they choose to allow it. God gives us free will. We always have the option to say no to God. For most abusers there is not enough personal incentive for them to change, and while God cares about us being abused, he won't force change upon our abusers against their will. What would the implications be if God forced people to repent?

To do

Make a happy jar to remind yourself that God cares enough to count your tears and collect them in a jar. Take an old glass jar and decorate it with tissue paper and PVA glue, or sequins or ribbons or anything else. Now find as many Bible verses as you can that remind you how much God cares about you. You can start with Psalm 56:8 and then see how many more you can find. Write each verse on a piece of paper, fold it up and fill the jar with those pieces of paper. Whenever you feel unloved, you can open your jar and read one of the verses to remind yourself of how precious you are to God.

Nice idea!

Section 2: How does abuse affect my relationship with God?

For I am convinced that neither death, nor life, nor angels, nor rulers, nor things present, nor things to come, nor powers, nor height, nor depth, nor anything else in all creation, will be able to separate us from the love of God in Christ Jesus our Lord. (Romans 8:38–39)

Every person's relationship with God is unique. Because we don't all experience domestic abuse in the same way, the effects of abuse on our faith will also vary from person to person. Those effects will be deeply personal and may take some time to explore and draw out, especially if we feel guilt or pain associated with them. It can sometimes be easier to consider the effects on our faith by hearing other people's stories. Looking at someone else's experiences from the outside in can help us frame what we've experienced.

Below are three stories. For each one, think about how the faith of the woman in the story could be affected by her situation.

Janet and Keith

Janet was a Christian and was married to Keith, who was not. At the beginning of the relationship, Keith said that Janet's faith was 'compelling'. He would go to church with her. In time, though, Keith began to ridicule Janet's faith. He called her a 'Bible basher' and said that her faith was a crutch for her emotional insecurities. He argued that he had gone to church with her and read the Bible for himself to give Christianity a chance, but anyone intelligent could see that it was all nonsense. At first Keith would encourage Janet to skip church, saying, 'Stay in bed with me', or, 'Let's go out for the day', but soon he started telling her it was a waste of time and she should be at home doing other things. If he saw Janet reading her Bible, he would take it away and tell her to get on with something useful. He got in a huff if he thought she was prioritising God over him.

How could Janet's faith have been affected by her situation?

Jane and Billy

Billy and Jane are both Christians. Billy was a worship leader, and Jane was a Sunday school teacher. When they met, Jane had been considering going into ministry, but Billy convinced her that women shouldn't preach. Billy and Jane would read the Bible together and listen to podcasts then discuss them. They went to all church events as a family. In the beginning Jane would not always agree with Billy's point of view, but he would not let debates rest and was so persistent that she began to defer to him as a biblical authority.

Billy said that women should submit, and the authority and priorities in a family should be: God first, man second, wife third, children fourth. Billy had a temper and would lose it when Jane 'nagged'. He said that it was better to sleep on the roof than with a nagging wife and that if she were a better Christian woman he wouldn't get so upset.

Jane was worried about her marriage and prayed about it for years. She read lots of Christian marriage books and was concentrating on being a better, more submissive, wife. She hoped that this would encourage Billy to be a kinder husband. She believed it was more important for her to remove the log from her own eye than focus on the speck in Billy's. She continued to forgive his outbursts. Jane spent a lot of time trying to make Billy happy, and most of her prayer time praying about her marriage.

How could Jane's relationship affect her faith?

Deborah and Mike

When Deborah met Mike, he told her he had just become a Christian. He'd had quite a colourful past, but he told her it was all behind him now. He said he had dedicated his life to Jesus. Mike had mental health problems and said he loved God but struggled with temptation and anger management issues. He said that this was why he had affairs and was violent towards Deborah.

Every so often Mike would say that he had lost his faith and refuse to go to church with Deborah. Their church attendance was sporadic, and Mike created an uncomfortable atmosphere at social events, so they didn't have many friends at church. Deborah felt as if they weren't considered 'good enough' Christians. They didn't have much involvement in any church activities outside of Sunday services. Mike never wanted to stay for coffee after the service. Services were often fraught, as they would have had an argument on the way there. Deborah hoped that Mike would grow in his faith and things would get better, and she regularly prayed for this. She wanted to support Mike through his mental health problems. However, when Mike would lose his faith, she often got distracted and forgot to pray or to read her Bible.

How might Deborah's situation affect her relationship with God?

To consider

As you can see from the hypothetical situations above, there are a variety of ways abuse can affect our relationship with God. Below is a list of some of the effects we might see. Tick any that you think might apply to you:

- [ ] My belief in God's existence has been undermined. I have doubts.
- [ ] I have been made to feel that I only have faith because I'm stupid or weak.
- [ ] I have been made to feel that my faith is not strong enough or good enough.
- [ ] I am unable to express my faith.
- [ ] I am embarrassed about my faith.
- [ ] I am unable to maintain fellowship with other Christians.
- [ ] I have begun to prioritise my husband over God.
- [ ] I do not use my spiritual gifts.
- [ ] I do not live to my full created potential.
- [ ] I am unable to discern for myself what I believe.
- [ ] I do not feel good enough for God.
- [ ] My prayer time is only ever about my marriage.
- [ ] I don't get to spend any time at all with God.
- [ ] I forget about God from time to time.
- [ ] I am distracted from God.
- [ ] I feel distant from God.
- [ ] I feel angry with God.
- [ ] I feel unloved and forgotten by God.
- [ ] I lack spiritual direction and growth.

Add below any other ways your relationship with God may have been affected.

Are there any thoughts or feelings that you have had towards God because of the abuse that you now think are untrue?

Jesus came to restore us to relationship with God. This is not just a supernatural restoration that will take place in the afterlife. It is real restoration here and now. There is no damage that abuse can do to your relationship with God that is irreparable. It can all be fixed through Christ. God *wants* a relationship with you. You may have been made to feel guilt and condemnation that you don't feel close to God, and that's something we will look at in chapter 7, but for now remember: whatever you have done, whatever has been done to you, there is no condemnation in Christ. God wants you to have fullness of life, and this is something you can have very real hope for.

To do

If you can, set some time apart to spend outdoors. That may be a walk in the woods, sitting on a beach watching the waves hit the shore, or a five-minute brew in the garden listening to the birds sing. Breathe deeply, let the peace of the fresh air and the quiet wash over you. There's something about the great outdoors that can refill a hungry soul and help us connect with God and with ourselves.

In her words

God gives us free choice. God can only transform someone who is willing to change. It's taken me a long time to realise that the abuse started the minute we married, and the more I submitted the more he took. I can look in the mirror and say, 'I've done everything I could.' I probably stayed longer because I was a Christian. I was angry with God that I'd done everything right and it had gone so wrong. Through the situation I have come to know so much more of God's love for me than I knew before.

(Anonymous survivor)

5

How am I affected by abuse?

Section 1: Grieving and coping

. . . we take every thought captive to obey Christ.
(2 Corinthians 10:5)

'What's the matter with you? You should be happy now that you're not being abused.' After leaving your abuser you may hear this message from those around you, but it's not that simple. Abuse strips us of so much, we need time to grieve. While we are grieving, we also have to deal with the effects of the abuse on our self-esteem and our ability to cope. We have a lot to recover from.

We must undertake the process of grieving when we suffer any major loss. Among those who haven't shared our experiences, there is a lack of understanding about this grief. This can make the process more difficult.

Consider what you have lost because of domestic abuse and write it in the space on the next page. In the space next to it consider what you have gained (or expect to gain) because of leaving the relationship.

Losses   **Gains**

Often, the things we lose when we leave an abusive relationship are immediate. We may lose physical belongings, our home, friends and maybe family. We may also have suffered loss of our sense of self and our self-esteem. We might lose the hopes and dreams we had for our future.

The things we gain, however, despite being arguably more important, tend to be longer-term. We can regain a stronger sense of self, more independence, better relationships, happiness, peace and more, but these things take time. In fact, when we first leave an abusive relationship, the gains can be difficult to imagine. They can seem amorphous, while our losses are tangible. Even our safety won't necessarily be an immediate reality, as we may have to take out non-molestation orders and injunctions. We may have to hide in a refuge or have extra security added to our home. The fear will not disappear overnight. It's unrealistic to expect survivors of domestic abuse to feel like celebrating when they first leave. We need to grieve first.

When we fall in love with an abuser, we fall in love with the person we believe they are. That person may not be real, but our feelings for them are. When we realise that the person we loved never really existed, and the life we imagined will never come to fruition, we need to grieve the loss of those things. The fact that they didn't exist doesn't make the grief any easier.

You may have heard of the stages of grief: denial, anger, bargaining, depression and acceptance. Allow yourself to experience these feelings; they are normal. Christians in particular can find anger a challenging emotion to deal with. We will be discussing that in more detail in chapter 8, but for now know that it is a normal and healthy part of the grieving process. The stages of grief are not linear: you need to grieve for each of those things you wrote in your losses list, so you might cycle around the different stages as you grieve different losses. You might also find yourself simultaneously feeling different stages of grief for different things. It's confusing to feel acceptance for something while still being angry about something else, but it is normal and healthy to work through these feelings.

For many survivors, domestic abuse has reinforced negative ways of thinking by making us feel perpetually horrible. Our feelings affect our thought processes, so if we're always feeling bad, we will start to continuously have negative thoughts. Our thought processes then affect our actions which, in turn, affect our feelings. It's easy to get stuck in a vicious cycle.

Have a look at the following examples and see if you can spot the feelings, thoughts and behaviours and how they affect each other:

- Sarah feels isolated and lonely. This makes her think that nobody likes her company, so after the church service she doesn't stay for coffee, but leaves without talking to anyone. This makes Sarah feel lonelier.
- Mary looks in the mirror and thinks she's fat and ugly. This makes her feel depressed. Mary comfort eats when she is depressed, gains weight and cannot fasten her jeans. This makes her think even more that she is fat and ugly.
- Joanna feels guilty. She feels guilty because she thinks she is a terrible mother. This makes her over-compensate with her children. She buys them gifts,

lets them stay up late, and doesn't set any boundaries. When Joanna realises that she has failed to set appropriate boundaries, she thinks, 'I have spoiled my children. I am a terrible mother.' She feels even more guilty.

The more we continue this negative cycle of thoughts, feelings and behaviour, the more we reinforce negative feelings until they become negative beliefs. This can happen to any person in any circumstance, and when it does, it's helpful to break the vicious cycle by changing the behaviour that is perpetuating it.

However, when we are in an abusive relationship this is not always possible. For example, we may realise we are becoming isolated and feeling as though people don't like us. We may realise that the healthiest thing to do in response is to push ourselves to go out and meet with friends, but our abuser may not allow us to do this. He may make it impossible, unsafe or not worth the consequences it will have on our life at home. This means we go longer without breaking the vicious cycle. Furthermore, our abuser may feed the negative thoughts. While we are feeling isolated and lonely we are more likely to believe him when he tells us that nobody likes us. This means that the negative feelings can become negative beliefs, and the negative behaviours can become habits. Even when we have left the relationship, it can be more difficult to recognise and break unhealthy thought patterns.

In the space on the next page write down the feelings that domestic abuse caused for you. For each of those feelings see if you can draw a vicious cycle to help you consider how those feelings may have affected your thought processes and behaviour. What can you do to break these vicious cycles?

When we experience trauma, we develop coping mechanisms in order to survive day to day. Coping mechanisms vary from person to person:

- We may work hard to normalise the situation to convince ourselves it's OK.
- We may use denial so that we don't have to admit even to ourselves that abuse is happening to us.
- We may keep the peace by becoming compliant and losing all our ability to assert ourselves.
- We may blame ourselves.
- We may physically or emotionally cut ourselves off from others.
- We may develop addictions.
- We may retreat into fantasy.
- We may become good at keeping secrets or telling lies.
- We may numb ourselves emotionally.

These coping strategies are a necessity for those in abusive relationships. However, when we leave, it may be that what started off as a coping strategy has become a habit and is no longer useful. These habits can become behaviours that then feed into negative thoughts and feelings, trapping us once again in a vicious cycle.

To consider

What coping strategies did you employ during your abusive relationship?

Have any of these coping strategies hung around and become habits?

If so, how might they feed into the vicious cycle?

To remember

Even if you have left an abusive relationship with a whole heap of negative thoughts and coping mechanisms that have become habits, you have survived and that is amazing. You are amazing!

Sometimes we are tempted to consider ourselves stupid or weak for having put up with things for whatever length of time we stayed. This is not justified. Remaining in an abusive relationship has nothing to do with intelligence or strength of character. Studies have shown that the psychological effects experienced by domestic abuse victims are similar to those of prisoners of war.[17]

Between these vicious cycles, the damage to self-esteem and unhelpful coping mechanisms, leaving your partner can feel impossible. If you've left, you have achieved something remarkable in and of itself – something many victims do not manage. You have survived trauma, and that takes an enormous amount of strength. Never forget that.

To do

Remind yourself how strong you are by writing a letter to yourself. Imagine that you are your best friend, and you want to offer some words of encouragement. Make sure that it bolsters and encourages you. You can go back and read it whenever you need a lift.

---

17 See, for example, Mary Romero, 'A comparison between strategies used on prisoners of war and battered wives', 1985, *Sex Roles: A Journal of Research*, *13*(9–10), 537–47.

Section 2: How I see myself

Finally, brothers and sisters, whatever is true, whatever is noble, whatever is right, whatever is pure, whatever is lovely, whatever is admirable – if anything is excellent or praiseworthy – think about such things. (Philippians 4:8, NIV)

When we spend time trapped in the vicious cycles we looked at in section 1, it can erode our sense of self. This leaves many of us feeling as if we just don't know who we are any more. Abusive partners often mould us into who they want us to be. We give way on the things that are important to us, and instead focus on being his 'other half'. As a result, we can forget who we are. In chapter 3 we looked at some of the beliefs about women that are foisted onto us by society. How do these beliefs and the effects of abuse make a difference to how we think about ourselves?

Opposite you will find four stick figures representing: a good Christian woman, a good Christian man, a sinful woman and a useless man. Write round each of these figures what you think their attributes will be. By this stage in your recovery, you may be more mindful of gender stereotypes, but for the purposes of this exercise, lean into stereotypes and go with the first reactions and thoughts that come to mind.

How am I affected by abuse?

Good Christian woman

Good Christian man

Good Christian woman

Good Christian man

Now compare the things you've written around the male and female figures. How are they similar and how do they differ? Are there particular attributes you associate with being female? Are there traits you associate with being male? Did you use negative words to describe the same attribute in one gender that you described positively in the other? For example, men may be described as 'strong' while women are described as 'pushy'; men may be 'leaders' while women are 'bossy'; women may be 'kind' but men 'soft'; women 'nurturing' and men 'effeminate'.

The language we use can feed into our attitudes about men and women, and therefore about ourselves. Our impression of what makes a 'good Christian woman' can affect the way we view our strengths and attributes. How do we see ourselves if we are not naturally maternal or nurturing? What if we possess leadership skills, strength or humour, but we don't consider these good traits in women? We tend to split human attributes into masculine and feminine and then judge ourselves harshly if we possess the 'wrong' ones. In reality, all traits are simply human traits, for better or worse.

Sometimes, we put pressure on ourselves to measure up to a picture of what an ideal Christian woman, wife or mother looks like. For those of us who have experienced abuse, this pressure can be amplified. We don't immediately stop feeling it when we leave. This image is often predicated on us completing a whole host of tasks, all cheerfully, while looking good (but not too sexy).

That pressure can also be applied by our abusers and their constant criticism, and some of this may be under the guise of church teachings. For example, we may have been given the passage about the wife of noble character from Proverbs 31 as a checklist of things we should live up to. However, the woman in Proverbs 31 didn't even exist. She was a fictional perfect woman used as a metaphor for wisdom. Proverbs 31 was written for men. In Jewish culture, men sing this proverb to their wives on Shabbat as an ode. It helps them to remember to honour and appreciate their wives; it was never written to be used as a 'to do' list for women. Basing your role as a wife on the Proverbs 31 woman is akin to basing your body image on Barbie: it's an impossible standard. Furthermore, what makes the woman in Proverbs 31 noble (or valiant) isn't the roles she fulfils or the long 'to do' list she achieves; it is her character. We know this because the Bible uses the same language to describe other, vastly different, women, such as Ruth and Rahab.[18]

Sometimes that pressure comes from comparison within church culture. Many of us turn up on a Sunday and put on our 'church face'. We pretend we have it all together. We don't share with one another when life is tough, because we see this as some kind of spiritual weakness. This isn't unique to women who have experienced abuse. In fact it's not unique to women. Our churches are filled with men and women who hide their brokenness from one another. It's easy to look around the pews at church and see only happy, joyful families. We fear authenticity, so we

18 There is a whole chapter devoted to Proverbs 31 in Rachel Held Evan's book, *A Year of Biblical Womanhood* (Nelson Books, 2012), or you can read more on this blog post: https://rachelheldevans.com/blog/mutuality-women-roles (accessed 23 November 2024).

hide mental health problems, addictions, family struggles, parenting challenges and all kinds of things we consider less savoury. The result is that when we go to church, we only see each other's curated lives. We feel surrounded by 'cookie-cutter' Christians all pretending to be the perfect Christian man or woman, when in fact we are a body of diverse and unique individuals, each created to shine in our own way.

It can be easy to compare our reality to this false impression and come away from church feeling that everyone else is blessed in ways we are not, or that they are better Christians than we are. We can try so hard, and for so long, to appear like that perfect Christian woman that we can completely lose sight of who we are uniquely created to be. No wonder so many of us say that we don't know who we are any more.

Jesus said that he didn't come for those who are perfect, but for those who are not doing so well: 'Those who are well have no need of a physician, but those who are sick. I have come to call not the righteous but sinners to repentance' (Luke 5:31–32). It's all right to be an imperfect Christian. We all are. Remember, we are made holy through Christ, not through being a 'good Christian woman'.

To consider

As a woman, do you feel good enough?

As a woman, do you feel pretty enough?

When you feel upset or angry, do you feel able to express it?

How does the notion that women are emotional, or the notion that women should be ladylike, affect you when you want to express anger?

Do you value your own strengths and abilities? If not, why not?

Are there any thoughts and feelings that you believed about yourself that you now know to be untrue and want to change?

What one habit or behaviour would you like to change in the next two months?

To do

Opposite is a scale by which you can measure your self-esteem.[19] For each statement, tick the box you feel most applies to you. Responses range from 'strongly agree' to 'strongly disagree'. When you've done this, add up the numbers in the boxes you ticked.

A score of 19–25 is considered to be within normal range; a score below 15 indicates low self-esteem. You could try this exercise again at the end of the book or simply in a few months' time, to see if your score has risen.

---

19 Adapted from Rosenberg's self-esteem scale.

How am I affected by abuse?

	Strongly agree	Agree	Disagree	Strongly disagree
I feel that I am a person worthy of God's love	3	2	1	0
I feel I am a unique contributor of God's kingdom with a number of good qualities	3	2	1	0
All in all I am inclined to feel I have let God down	0	1	2	3
I am able to endure all things in Christ's strength	3	2	1	0
I feel I do not have much to be proud of	0	1	2	3
I take a positive attitude towards myself	3	2	1	0
On the whole I think God is pleased and proud of me	3	2	1	0
I wish I could have more respect for myself	0	1	2	3
I certainly feel useless at times	0	1	2	3
At times I feel I have much to be ashamed of	0	1	2	3

In her words

My head
Tense, tight, pain, pressure.
The memories.
The flashbacks.
The critical unkind words.
I go back, I feel the pain.
Back again, another memory, I feel the pain.

I travel in time.
Years of memories and pain.
Stored in a bookshelf.
Shelves reaching to the ceiling.
Books full of stories telling my life.

I walk through the woods.
The sun warming my face, calming my mind.
The birds alive, singing the sound eases the pain.
The sound of my boots on the path.
The rhythm, the sound,
One, two, one, two.

I walk, I breathe.
I am here.
I am now.
The memory comes.
I feel the sun.
I hear the birds.
I feel the ground.
There is healing.
(Caroline, 2019)

Bible study 2
Just the helper?

Then the LORD God said, 'It is not good that the man should be alone; I will make him a helper as his partner.'
(Genesis 2:18)

What springs to mind when you read the word 'helper' in this Bible verse?

If you've ever been to a concert, you've probably listened to a support act. The support act isn't usually as exciting as the main event. Many concert-goers don't even bother to turn up until they know it's time for the main event. The job of the support act is to help the headline artist by warming up the crowd, getting them excited for what is to come. This is how many Christians see a woman's role in relation to a man's. As the 'helpers', they think we're the support act, while the men are the main event. They think we're here to further their mission and calling, by supporting and cheering for them.

The two-word phrase in the Bible translated from the Hebrew as 'helper' is *ezer kenegdo*. This isn't the only time the word *ezer* appears in the Old Testament. It's more frequently used to describe God as a helper, for example in Psalm 121:1–2, when it says: 'I lift up my eyes to the hills – from where will my help come? My help comes from the LORD, who made heaven and earth.' Or in Psalm 46:1, where it says: 'God is our refuge and strength, a very present help in trouble.' Or if that's not enough to convince you, look up Deuteronomy 33, where the same word is used to describe God in verses 7, 26 and 29.

Does this kind of helper seem like a support act?

What qualities make God our very present help in times of need?

If God is described as our helper, and Eve is also described as Adam's helper, what does that suggest about Adam and Eve's relationship?

As well as referring to God, the word *ezer* is sometimes used in the Old Testament to describe the nations that Israel had relied on for military aid. This military metaphor can also be seen in the descriptions of God when God is described as our shield and sword, a protector and defender who rides across the heavens to our aid. An *ezer* is not a support act. An *ezer* is a warrior! *Ezer* is also sometimes translated as 'strong', such as in Psalm 89:19 in the NIV, where it says: 'Once you spoke in a vision, to your faithful people you said: "I have bestowed strength on a warrior; I have raised up a young man from among the people."'

Although the word 'helper' isn't an incorrect translation, the way we think of a helper today does not align with its original meaning. We wouldn't dream of referring to God as 'just a helper', but the same language is used for Eve in her relationship to Adam. Eve is Adam's help in the same way that God is all of humanity's help. God is the one we turn to because we cannot manage in our own strength. God is the one who rescues and delivers. God is the one whose strength is necessary for us to be able to complete our task. Not as a secondary assistant to the main jobholder, but as a strong warrior.

You could almost be forgiven for reading the word *ezer* and instead of thinking that Eve was inferior to Adam, thinking she must have been superior. After all, this is a word used to describe God. This is where *kenegdo* comes in.

Kenegdo means 'to be in perfect harmony' or 'to be perfectly balanced'. Imagine a scale with weights either side, each weight exactly the same so the scale is completely even. Another way to understand the term is to imagine two oxen pulling a cart. If the oxen are not equal in strength and ability, and they do not pull in the same direction, the load will come under uneven pressure, the cart will break and the oxen could be injured. This is where the biblical phrase 'equally yoked' comes from.

Eve was Adam's help, neither as an inferior nor a superior but as an equal. *Kenegdo* is often translated as 'suitable'. You may have heard the phrase 'a suitable helper', but in our modern understanding of 'suitable helper', it's not an ideal translation. A better translation in today's language might be 'I will make a strong and equal partner to help him.'

Compare the account of the creation of humankind in Genesis 2 to the account in Genesis 1. Reading Genesis 1 from verse 26 onwards, count how many times you read the word 'them'.

Then God said, 'Let us make humankind in our image, according to our likeness; and let *them* have dominion over the fish of the sea, and over the birds of the air, and over the cattle, and over all the wild animals of the earth, and over every creeping thing that creeps upon the earth.' So God created humankind in his image, in the image of God he created *them*; male and female he created *them*. God blessed *them*, and God said to *them*, 'Be fruitful and multiply, and fill the earth and subdue it; and have dominion over the fish of the sea and over the birds of the air and over every living thing that moves upon the earth.' God said, 'See, I have given you every plant yielding seed that is upon the face of all the earth, and every tree with seed in its fruit; you shall have them for food. And to every beast of the earth, and to every bird of the air, and to everything that creeps on the earth, everything that has the breath of life, I have given every green plant for food.' And it was so. God saw everything that he had made, and indeed, it was very good. And there was evening and there was morning, the sixth day. (Genesis 1:26–31, my emphasis)

There is no distinction made between man and woman: God created *them*, both of them, equally in God's image. God gave them dominion over the earth, told them to be fruitful and subdue the earth. God blessed them.

Men and women, from the point of creation, are shown to be fully equal in worth, in role and in blessing, and this is described as 'very good'.

To consider

What do the words *ezer kenegdo* tell you about God's intention when he created women?

What does it tell you about your potential?

What do you think it means to be equally yoked?

Do you think differently about God's intention for marriage after studying this passage anew?

In her words

I found being in a new relationship with a widow who had had a healthy marriage was very healing and restoring. God used this to show me that my 'normal' was actually pretty abnormal. I also realised I was attractive, and I challenged the lie that I was unlovable.

(Anonymous survivor)

Moving

My notes

My notes

6

Who am I in Christ?

Section 1: God's child

He will rejoice over you with gladness, he will renew you in his love; he will exult over you with loud singing.
(Zephaniah 3:17)

One Sunday morning, I found myself looking around church during one of the hymns. On the row in front of me was an old woman, too frail to stand for the singing – she worshipped in her seat. Across the aisle a mother stood cradling her baby. I couldn't help but smile as I watched her holding her daughter close, rocking her to the sound of the music, gazing at her with love as she sang. It was a beautiful picture of unconditional maternal love.

As I watched her, I thought about how our timeless God sees this precious child. God is timeless; God sees her whole life. God also sees her at the age of the elderly woman on the row in front, perhaps time-weathered and exhausted, but smiling and singing nonetheless.

Whatever this child will become, God sees it all: each step, each struggle, every person she'll love, every success she'll celebrate, the cruel words she will speak, and the callous thoughts that will cross her mind. God has already collected all the tears she will shed in a jar. Every day of this child's life is written in God's book, the good and the bad. Every. Single. Thing. God knows her, all of her. And yet God gazes at her with the same unconditional love that I saw on her mother's face. God loves her. She is God's little girl.

This reminded me that God looks at me in the same way: as the youngest baby in her family, born after years of trying; as the annoying five-year-old drawing on her sisters' homework; as the muddled teenager, the scared student, the newlywed full of hope, the exhausted new mum; as the victim huddled on the floor cradling her bruised body. God sees all my anger, my grief, my tears, my joy and my heart so overflowing with love for those around me that I sometimes think it might burst. God sees my future; God looks at me now and sees achievements and failures I haven't even considered. God sees all the sins I will commit. God sees the people I will love and the tears I'll shed for them. God sees me facing future adversity and knows whether or not I'll do so with dignity. God sees that point when my body will break, when life will leave me and I'll breathe my last. All of it. Good, bad and everything in between. God sees it, sees me, completely, all at once. And it fills God's heart with joy.

As I looked around church that morning at people praising God, I saw young and old, black and white, rich and poor. I was suddenly overwhelmed by the joy they all bring to God as God looks on their lives, their entire lives, the sum total of everything they are and will ever be, so vastly different from each other, so flawed and imperfect and wonderful. All loved, in their completeness, by their Creator. All loved in the way a mother loves her infant child.

You are God's little girl, no matter what has happened in your life, no matter what you have done and no matter what has been done to you. In the previous chapter we thought about the pressure we sometimes put on ourselves to be 'good Christian women', but when God looks upon us, that isn't what God is looking at. God doesn't look at what we do, but rather, the Bible tells us, 'the LORD looks on the heart' (1 Samuel 16:7).

God looks at our heart and sees it as completely reconciled to God's heart, because we are seen in the light of Jesus' work of salvation. Remember that God has removed our sins from us 'as far as the east is from the west' (Psalm 103:12). God simply doesn't see our sins when looking at us.

There is sometimes a misconception that God is too holy to look upon us, or cannot stand to be in our presence because of our sin. This is not true. First of all, it's not true because of Jesus. Jesus has dealt with our sin, all of it, for all time. Hence why God doesn't see it. But even before Jesus, even before you were saved, God loved you. Ephesians 1:4 says we were chosen, in love, before the foundations of the world were even laid. Romans 5:8 says that God loved us 'while we still were sinners'. Even when we are in a sinful state, we are loved deeply by God. Our sin may affect our relationship with God, but it cannot separate us from God's love. In fact, as we read earlier, 'neither death, nor life, nor angels, nor rulers, nor things present, nor things to come, nor powers, nor height, nor depth, nor anything else in all creation, will be able to separate us from the love of God in Christ Jesus our Lord' (Romans 8:38–39).

When people quote the Bible saying that God is too holy to look upon us in our sinful state, they are usually quoting the Old Testament prophets. They would lament the sins of Israel and ask why a holy God still loved the people. For example, in Habakkuk 1:13, it says: 'Your eyes are too pure to behold evil, and you cannot look on wrongdoing; why do you look on the treacherous and are silent when the wicked swallow those more righteous than they?' Habakkuk was essentially saying, 'You are too holy to look upon sin, so why do you?' It was difficult for the prophets to comprehend why a good God had so much time and love for sinful humans. It is hard for us to comprehend that too, but the Bible tells us that, no matter how hard it is for us to understand, we are indeed deeply loved by God.

To consider

In the blank space below, create something to show what God sees when looking at you. It can be a list, a poem, a picture – whatever works for you. The list of Bible verses will help you with considering God's view of humanity.

Now look at the list of Bible verses again and, for each one, ask yourself if you believe these things about yourself.

- 'But to all who believed him and accepted him, he gave the right to become children of God' (John 1:12, NLT).
- 'For we are God's masterpiece. He has created us anew in Christ Jesus, so we can do the good things he planned for us long ago' (Ephesians 2:10, NLT).
- 'Now all of us can come to the Father through the same Holy Spirit because of what Christ has done for us' (Ephesians 2:18, NLT).
- 'So you also are complete through your union with Christ, who is the head over every ruler and authority' (Colossians 2:10, NLT).
- 'Therefore, there is now no condemnation for those who are in Christ Jesus, because through Christ Jesus the law of the Spirit who gives life has set you free from the law of sin and death' (Romans 8:1-2, NIV).
- 'For I am convinced that neither death, nor life, nor angels, nor rulers, nor things present, nor things to come, nor powers, nor height, nor depth, nor anything else in all creation, will be able to separate us from the love of God in Christ Jesus our Lord' (Romans 8:38-39).
- 'Being confident of this, that he who began a good work in you will carry it on to completion until the day of Christ Jesus' (Philippians 1:6, NIV).
- 'But our citizenship is in heaven. And we eagerly await a Saviour from there, the Lord Jesus Christ' (Philippians 3:20, NIV).

- 'For the Spirit God gave us does not make us timid, but gives us power, love and self-discipline' (2 Timothy 1:7, NIV).
- 'You are the light of the world. A town built on a hill cannot be hidden' (Matthew 5:14, NIV).
- 'You did not choose me, but I chose you and appointed you so that you might go and bear fruit – fruit that will last – and so that whatever you ask in my name the Father will give you' (John 15:16, NIV).
- 'Don't you know that you yourselves are God's temple and that God's Spirit lives among you?' (1 Corinthians 3:16, NIV).
- 'Therefore, if anyone is in Christ, the new creation has come: the old has gone, the new is here!' (2 Corinthians 5:17, NIV).

To do

One way we can address negative thought patterns is to train our brain into thinking more positively about ourselves. We can do this by repeating a positive affirmation to ourselves every day. The more we hear negative thoughts, the more likely they are to become beliefs. In the same way, the more we hear positive thoughts, the more likely they are to become our beliefs. These affirmations have to be grounded in reality so that they are believable.

Have another look at the exercise you did exploring how God sees humanity. Use this to create an affirmation. Write it somewhere you will see it every day – perhaps pin it to your fridge, stick it on your mirror or put it on a bookmark. Then say it out loud to yourself every day this week.

Some examples of affirmations are:

- I am a beloved daughter of God.
- God delights over me with singing.
- God has empowered me to do good things in God's name.
- I am strong and capable.

What will your affirmation be this week?

Section 2: Self-esteem and setting boundaries

We are God's masterpiece. He has created us anew in Christ Jesus, so we can do the good things he planned for us long ago.
(Ephesians 2:10, NLT)

How did you score on the self-esteem scale in chapter 5? Do you see yourself as God sees you? Do you have healthy self-esteem? Does it even matter?

Focusing on loving ourselves can be challenging for Christian women, because we are taught to be humble and to serve others. The Bible tells us to 'do nothing from selfish ambition or conceit, but in humility regard others as better than yourselves' (Philippians 2:3). Some Christians mistakenly consider healthy and accurate self-esteem to be prideful.

In the circles on the following pages, imagine four planets and write in those circles the kind of behaviour you would expect to see on each.

Planet Healthy Self-Esteem

Here everyone believes they are loved, chosen and made holy through Christ.

Planet Low Self-Esteem

Here everyone believes they are inherently bad and unlikeable.

Planet Serving

Here everyone seeks to put the needs of others before themselves.

Planet Selfish

Here everyone puts themselves first.

Which planet would you like to live on? I imagine it's Planet Healthy Self-Esteem, where everyone believes they are loved and chosen. There, the insecurities that lead to a lot of unkind behaviour would be a thing of the past. Also, the global self-confidence would free everyone from limiting beliefs, so they could truly fulfil the purpose God had designed for them. In a world where people believed they were loved and chosen by their Creator, they would surely feel a sense of gratitude and pay this forward. I imagine, then, that Planet Healthy Self-Esteem would look fairly similar to Planet Serving.

In contrast, on Planet Low Self-Esteem, where people felt unlikeable and unlovable, they wouldn't have the confidence to live their lives to the full. They wouldn't want to serve others, and might be frightened of getting things wrong. It's likely that the planet's residents wouldn't be fun to be around and would selfishly wallow in self-pity.

Our self-esteem has a knock-on effect on those around us. Healthy self-esteem is not selfish. In fact, it's a necessity if we're going to serve others. Without it, our well-being can be severely damaged and that hinders our ability to support those around us. We can't keep others well if we are not well ourselves. Rick Warren wrote: 'Humility is not thinking less of yourself; it is thinking of yourself less. Humility is thinking more of others.'[20] Humility and self-esteem are not mutually exclusive. Self-esteem tells me, 'I am a beloved masterpiece of the creator of the universe.' Humility tells me, 'So is everyone else.'

---

20 Rick Warren, *The Purpose Driven Life* (Grand Rapids: Zondervan, 2007).

Do you believe you were created for a purpose? Genesis tells us that, as humans, we were created in the image of God. Our purpose is to reflect our Creator. It takes all of humanity to reflect God's immense glory. Just as each facet of a diamond reflects the light differently, causing the diamond to sparkle, every human who ever existed and ever will exist reflects a different facet of God. For God's glory to shine brightly, we all need to reflect God in our own unique way. We need to let the light of our original design from God shine from within us. How do we do that? By being our individual, created, wonderful selves. If we have low self-esteem and fail to recognise our unique, God-given beauty, we fail to recognise our Creator's good work.

To consider

What is the difference between low self-esteem and humility?

What is the difference between healthy self-esteem and pride?

What is unique and beautiful about you?

Just as a mistaken understanding of humility can make it difficult for us to work on our self-esteem, a mistaken understanding of service can make it difficult for Christian women to set boundaries. For those of us who have experienced domestic abuse, this can be worse, as it's not always been safe for us to set boundaries. This could mean we have developed habits that make saying no difficult.

When we have healthy self-esteem, and believe we are a person of worth with important needs, setting boundaries starts to become a little easier. It's important to remember that setting boundaries isn't selfish. In fact, it is an essential act of self-care that can ensure we have the energy we need to serve others. Jesus regularly set boundaries; he withdrew from the crowds to go to quiet places when he needed time alone (Luke 5:15–16). He said no to the disciples when they had a different agenda in mind (Matthew 16:23). He said no to his mother and brothers when they tried to use their relationship with him to pull him away from the crowds (Matthew 12:46–50). And he said no to Herod when he asked him to provide a sign that he was the Son of God (Luke 23:8–9). Jesus modelled healthy boundaries in his life and teaching.

Here are some top tips for setting boundaries:

- If you struggle to say no immediately, delay your decision, saying something like, 'I'll check my diary and let you know.'
- Practise what you're going to say beforehand. It may feel crazy to rehearse conversations with yourself in your head, but it's not! Practice makes perfect!
- Use the broken-record technique: if someone isn't responding the first time you set a boundary, don't be afraid to repeat your message until it's been heard.
- If you're addressing a behaviour you dislike, focus your comments on the behaviour and how it makes you feel rather than on the personal qualities of the person you are speaking to. For example, to say, 'When you leave your underpants on the bathroom floor and I have to pick them up, it makes me feel taken advantage of', is better than, 'Why do you have to be so messy?'
- Remember Matthew 5:37, 'Let your "Yes" be "Yes," and

your "No," "No"' (NKJV). It is enough to simply say no. You don't have to give lengthy explanations.

To do

Plant a seed or a bulb in a small pot. Over the next few weeks and months, nurture your seed and watch it grow. What does it need? It needs care, it needs water, sunlight and space. If you were to plant too many seeds in one pot, they would become overwhelmed by each other and wouldn't grow.

Like the plant, you need space to grow. Setting boundaries with people gives you this space. Boundaries don't just offer protection from inappropriate behaviour; they give us the space we need to flourish, to grow, to become ourselves.

As you nurture your plant, consider how you can also nurture yourself.

In her words

I had no idea who I was. One day before he left, I curled up in a ball in a spare bedroom and sobbed and sobbed like I would never stop. I remember thinking and muttering, 'Who am I? What has happened? What was I?' Rebuilding myself has meant I've gone back to the person I was as a child, a young person and an adult until ten years ago when I met the perpetrator. I dug out old toys and clothes and photos and mementos, and concentrated on that 'me'. I restarted the interests I had in those years. I threw out all books, music, clothes and photos that had a connection with the perpetrator. My house and I now feel like 'me'. I am still fragile, but it is so good to be me.

(Anonymous survivor)

Bible study 3

What does it mean to submit?

Be subject to one another out of reverence for Christ.

Wives, be subject to your husbands as you are to the Lord. For the husband is the head of the wife just as Christ is the head of the church, the body of which he is the Saviour. Just as the church is subject to Christ, so also wives ought to be, in everything, to their husbands.

Husbands, love your wives, just as Christ loved the church and gave himself up for her, in order to make her holy by cleansing her with the washing of water by the word, so as to present the church to himself in splendour, without a spot or wrinkle or anything of the kind – yes, so that she may be holy and without blemish. In the same way, husbands should love their wives as they do their own bodies. He who loves his wife loves himself. For no one ever hates his own body, but he nourishes and tenderly cares for it, just as Christ does for the church, because we are members of his body.

(Ephesians 5:21–30)

Pliny the Younger, a prominent writer from the first century, *hated* the new emerging religion that would later become known as Christianity. He called it a 'depraved and excessive superstition'. His disapproval was due to Christians not respecting the household codes of Roman society.[21]

The household codes were more than just social norms. They were legally instituted ways of living that all Roman households were obligated, by law, to adhere to. The Romans believed that household codes were crucial to the smooth functioning of society as a whole. Men were expected to unilaterally rule over their households, because slaves, women and children were all considered to be inferior to men.

Christianity turned this thinking on its head, and as a result it was considered the religion of women and slaves. So why then would Paul be reinforcing those household codes by telling women to submit to their husbands? The answer can be found in verse 21.

Who was Ephesians 5:21 aimed at?

---

21 Beth Allison Barr shares this Pliny the Younger quote, as well as several other quotes from Roman and Jewish historians, about the household codes. She details Ephesians 5, as well as several other portions of Paul's writings that have been wrongly weaponised against women. See Beth Allison Barr, *The Making of Biblical Womanhood* (Brazos Press, 2021), chapter 2.

When Paul says, 'Be subject to one another', are there any exclusions?

Paul subverts the Roman household codes by asking *all* members to submit to one another. For women the instruction here is simple: 'Be subject to your husbands as you are to the Lord.' In other words: carry on doing what you're already doing, but not because of your husband's authority, but rather because of Jesus' authority. The instructions to husbands, however, are far more radical and counter-cultural. Note that the instructions to wives about submission take up three verses (verses 22–24), but the instructions to husbands about submitting to their wives take up more than twice that number (verses 25–31). Paul is far more concerned with giving clear instructions to husbands about what their submission should look like.

How does Ephesians 5:24 onwards suggest a man should submit to his wife?

Paul tells men to submit to their wives in the same way that Jesus loves the Church. If the man is to be to his wife as Christ is to the Church, what will that look like? What examples can we find of Christ submitting to the Church?

There are several examples of Christ submitting his own will and acting as a servant to his followers; for example, when he washed the disciples' feet. But perhaps the most notable example of submission by Christ is the incarnation itself, where Jesus lays aside all the power and authority of God and submits himself to life as a vulnerable human, for our sake. When we look at Paul's letter to the Ephesians, instructing men to behave as Christ did, we should remember that Paul also wrote:

> Let the same mind be in you that was in Christ Jesus, who, though he was in the form of God, did not regard equality with God as something to be exploited, but emptied himself, taking the form of a slave, being born in human likeness. And being found in human form, he humbled himself and became obedient to the point of death – even death on a cross.
> (Philippians 2:5–8)

This is the submission Paul was instructing men to show to their wives. Jesus, as God, held the ultimate position of authority over humanity, but he chose to give that up. Behaving like Christ does not mean wielding power and authority; it means relinquishing power and authority. Paul did not place husbands in a position of authority over their wives. Rather, he recognised that men already held authority, given to them by society, and he told them to lay that authority aside, just as Jesus had done.

Do these instructions for husbands leave any room for abusive behaviour?

Rachel Held Evans writes:

When put into practice, these Christianized household codes would break down, rather than reinforce, the hierarchal boundaries between husband and wife, master and slave, adult parent and adult child. If wives submit to their husbands as the Church submits to Christ (Ephesians 5:24), and if husbands love their wives as Christ loved the Church and gave himself up for her (Ephesians 5:25), and if both husbands and wives, slaves and masters submit one to another (Ephesians 5:21) – who's really 'in charge' here?[22]

So, do we need to submit to our husbands? Yes, and they should submit to us too. Submission does not mean making ourselves inferior or placing ourselves under another's authority. It certainly does not mean that we should put up with bad behaviour or being treated as though we are 'less than' the other person. Rather, submission is simply the act of putting the other person first, and in a healthy relationship we should expect such behaviour to be reciprocated. What does biblical submission look like, and who should we submit to?

---

22 Rachel Held Evans, 'Aristotle vs. Jesus: What makes the New Testament household codes different?' 28 August 2013 at: https://rachelheldevans.com/blog/aristotle-vs-jesus-what-makes-the-new-testament-household-codes-different (accessed 9 December 2024).

In her words

Jesus came to bring freedom and bind up the broken-hearted. I can say he truly has in my case! When I first got out, I felt lost and adrift, without a rudder. All I had hoped for had been smashed to bits. Growing up in the Church, I believed you weren't allowed to get divorced, except in cases of adultery and an unbelieving spouse. Neither of which applied to me! But how could God forgive sins like prostitution and murder but be so strict about divorce and remarriage? God's heart is always to protect and provide for the widow and fatherless – not further condemn and shackle.

If you are in an abusive relationship, God wants you and your children safe and emotionally whole. Get out and stay out. Can God redeem situations? Absolutely! But where there are serious issues of unequal power and control, staying in the situation just gives the controller more power. If someone fell into a pit of poisonous snakes, you wouldn't tell them they had to stay there, would you? But that's effectively what some Christian leaders naively say.

(Anonymous survivor)

My notes

My notes

7

When will I stop feeling guilty?

Section 1: Religious guilt and abuse

If the Son makes you free, you will be free indeed.
(John 8:36)

I'm a failed breastfeeder. I valiantly tried for six weeks, but my eldest child just didn't ever latch on properly. At one midnight feed, as the pain in my bleeding nipples became too much, I gave up and made the switch to formula milk. It was the best choice for me and my baby. It also left me riddled with guilt.

This was my first experience of the particular type of guilt that I've felt in relation to my children. Some people call it 'mum guilt'. I call it 'permaguilt', because it never goes away. The thing with 'permaguilt' is that there's always something to feel guilty about. If I choose to go back to work, I feel guilty for abandoning my child; if I choose to be a stay-at-home mum, I feel guilty for not making a financial contribution to the household. If I buy toys for my child, I feel guilty for spoiling them; if I don't buy them a toy, I feel guilty for being mean. If I feed them frozen chips and chicken nuggets, I feel guilty for not providing a healthy diet; if I give them vegetables, I feel guilty for giving them food I know they will refuse to eat. Sometimes, as a mother, it's easy to feel you're doing everything wrong. I'm also sure this feeling of 'permaguilt' isn't exclusive to mothers.

For Christian women, this kind of guilt can be compounded by 'religious guilt'. As Christians, we often feel that we should uphold a higher standard than the rest of the world. We know we are supposed to be salt and light, and as such we may feel we have to follow a particular moral code. When we fail to achieve the high standards we hold ourselves to, or when we feel we are not living up to them as well as others are, it can easily lead to feelings of guilt, condemnation and shame.

Think about some of the rules that you may have imposed on yourself or that may have been imposed on you by others within the Christian community. Some of these rules may come directly from the Bible; others may be cultural. At the moment, we are not considering whether these rules are right or wrong. We are just thinking about what rules we may have felt we should follow.

Here are a few of mine to get you started. In the space on the next page, add your own to this list.

- Do not wear short skirts.
- Do not swear.
- Do not have sex outside of marriage.
- Do not go shopping on a Sunday.
- Do not blaspheme/take the Lord's name in vain.
- Do not get drunk.
- Do not be alone with a man who is not your husband.

How does this list make you feel?

Regardless of whether we believe these are good rules to live by or not, it can seem that being a Christian comes with a whole list of restrictions. When we attempt to apply long, exhaustive and stringent lists of rules to our lives, it is inevitable that we will fail. We are human, and as such we experience temptation. The more something is not allowed, the more we will be tempted. The more we are tempted, the harder we will find it to resist. When we fail, we feel guilt and shame. Is this the freedom that Christ came to bring us? Is this what abundance of life looks like?

While Jesus did not come to overturn the law, he did come to set us free from it. The law represents God's morality. Jesus does not overturn morality, but gives us a better way to make moral choices. He doesn't simply insist we follow inflexible rules that often serve no purpose other than to make us feel guilty. As we saw in our first Bible study, Jesus told us in Matthew 22 that if we put love at the centre of all we do, we will naturally make good moral choices without the need for hundreds of imposing and shaming rules.

Go back through the list of rules you wrote and consider which of these are a natural outworking of love. For example, with the rule 'do not steal', if I really love my neighbour, then I don't need a rule to tell me not to steal from them. I won't do it, because that's not a loving thing to do. Don't forget that we ought to show love to ourselves as well, so some rules may be a natural outworking of taking care of ourselves; for example, resting on the Sabbath. When we use love as our guideline rather than a hard-and-fast rule, it also allows us to understand that it's the spirit of the rule that matters, not the rule itself, and as such there may be occasions when we need to break a rule. Jesus broke the rule about working on the Sabbath in order to heal people, because, on that occasion, it was the most loving course of action. We do not need to feel guilty about breaking religious rules if we have done so in order to pursue the most loving response, be that towards someone else or towards ourselves.

When you've highlighted the rules that are a natural outworking of love, consider what is left. Are these rules biblically based, or are they man-made and cultural? Do they help you to love your neighbour better or to become more like Jesus? Or do they send you on unnecessary guilt trips? Cross out the rules that serve no purpose other than to make you feel guilt and shame. You don't need these in your life.

We can look at society and see the reasons why so many women experience 'mum guilt'. Stories in the media blame mothers when children go off the rails or get hurt. Advertising and social media pressurise mothers into competitive parenting and comparison. Even our social care system tends to encourage parenting courses as solutions before offering support. Similarly, we can look at Christian culture and see reasons why Christians may feel 'religious guilt', be it the imposition of rules, the 'othering' of those on the edges, or the cookie-cutter 'perfect Christian' lie we tell each other that we discussed in the last chapter.

All of the societal and religious pressures, rules and comparisons that can lead to women feeling guilty are a gift to perpetrators of abuse. When we feel guilt and shame, we are much easier to control – we work harder to make things right. This is why abusers often use religious rules and teachings or societal notions of what makes a good woman to apply more guilt and more shame. They may also impose their own rules for the household, which will inevitably shift and change so that we cannot keep them even if we try. They will then blame us for the abuse when we break the rules, by saying things such as, 'Look what you made me do', or, 'If only you would . . . then I wouldn't have to do this.' If we are already feeling guilty it's easier for an abuser to feed into that and blame us for his behaviour.

Sometimes when we feel guilt it is because we have genuinely done something wrong, and we need to take action to put that right. We will be looking at those situations in the next section. But more often than not, especially when we have experienced abuse, we accept blame for situations that are not our fault, or we feel guilty for things that are not wrong. None of us should feel guilty for the abusive behaviour of our partner. That behaviour was his choice and his responsibility. None of us should feel guilty for making choices to keep ourselves and our children safe from domestic abuse. That's just a guilt trip. None of us should feel guilty for spending money on ourselves or doing something nice for ourselves from time to time. Taking care of yourself is not selfish; it's necessary.

To consider

How did your abuser use guilt to control you?

Did your abuser use your religious convictions to make you feel bad?

How did this make you feel about yourself?

What effects has guilt had on your life?

To do

Write down on a piece of paper anything you feel guilty about. Then consider that guilt. Is it really something that warrants your guilt, or is it just something that's causing you to send yourself on a guilt trip?

For anything that falls into the latter category, make a conscious decision not to allow yourself to dwell on it or feel guilty about it any more. Whenever you think of it, use logic to remind yourself that you have nothing to feel guilty for.

Now take that piece of paper and destroy it: shred it, tear it up or (safely) burn it. This thing is not going to have a hold over you any more.

Section 2: Dealing with guilt

There is therefore now no condemnation for those who are in Christ Jesus.
(Romans 8:1)

After reading the first section of this chapter you may find yourself asking: 'Isn't guilt simply the pricking of our conscience, or the way we feel when the Holy Spirit convicts us of our sin, so that we can repent?'

Of course there will be times when we mess up and make mistakes, and God convicts us of this. However, the guilt trips we have discussed so far are not conviction; they are condemnation. Condemnation is when we feel shame for something we have no need to feel guilty about, or for something we have already repented of and been forgiven for.

The Bible tells us that 'God did not send the Son into the world to condemn the world, but in order that the world might be saved through him' (John 3:17). We are not supposed to feel condemnation. Sometimes we repent and we know we are forgiven but we still feel a nagging sense of shame, because we haven't forgiven ourselves, or perhaps we don't really believe deep down that we have been forgiven. The Bible tells us:

The LORD is merciful and gracious, slow to anger and abounding in steadfast love. He will not always accuse, nor will he keep his anger for ever. He does not deal with us according to our sins, nor repay us according to our iniquities. For as the heavens are high above

the earth, so great is his steadfast love towards those who fear him; as far as the east is from the west, so far he removes our transgressions from us.
(Psalm 103:8–12)

We don't need to feel any shame for things we have repented of, because they are no longer part of us. God has completely removed them and does not see them when looking at us.

And yet, as humans, we are prone to feeling condemnation. It's helpful then to be able to recognise whether that little voice inside your head, telling you that you've messed up, is conviction (the Holy Spirit pricking your conscience), or condemnation (the voice of shame).

Here are some differences between the two:

Conviction focuses on the behaviour ('I shouldn't have . . .).	Condemnation focuses on the person ('I'm a bad person').
Conviction demands that we apologise and make retribution (if possible) to the person we have sinned against.	Condemnation makes us feel as though we are hated and have destroyed our relationship; it makes us want to hide away.
Conviction encourages us to take responsibility.	Condemnation encourages us to feel shame and to cover up our mistakes.

Conviction reminds us that we are dearly loved, even when we mess up.	Condemnation makes us feel worthless.
Conviction goes away once we've repented.	Condemnation lingers like a bad smell.
Conviction leads to freedom.	Condemnation leads to shame.

When we live in condemnation, we are prevented from living the fullness of life we are promised in Christ. It robs us of our joy, damages our self-esteem and prevents us from growing in Christ. Condemnation affects our relationship with God and with others. It allows abusers to control us and leads us to make poor choices. Condemnation prevents us from taking full advantage of God's good gift of grace, so how do we defeat it?

One way to avoid condemnation is to deal properly with conviction so that we don't fall into a cycle of shame. Take a look at the diagram on the following page.

Just as we can get trapped in cycles of negative thinking and feeling, we can become trapped in cycles of shame. We do something that goes against our own values, and this leads to feelings of guilt and shame, then we react to those feelings in often unhealthy ways. For example, we may cover up what we did wrong, or we may make bad choices to try to overcompensate for that mistake. These reactions lead to further feelings of shame and negative thoughts about ourselves. When we're thinking badly of ourselves we are more likely to repeat poor behaviours, and so the cycle continues.

We can break the cycle at any point. When we have negative feelings, we can remind ourselves that we are loved, even when we make mistakes. We can choose to react to those feelings by apologising and making amends where possible. Even if we fail again and react badly, we can work on our negative thoughts, again reminding ourselves that it's OK to be human and mess up. We are forgiven.

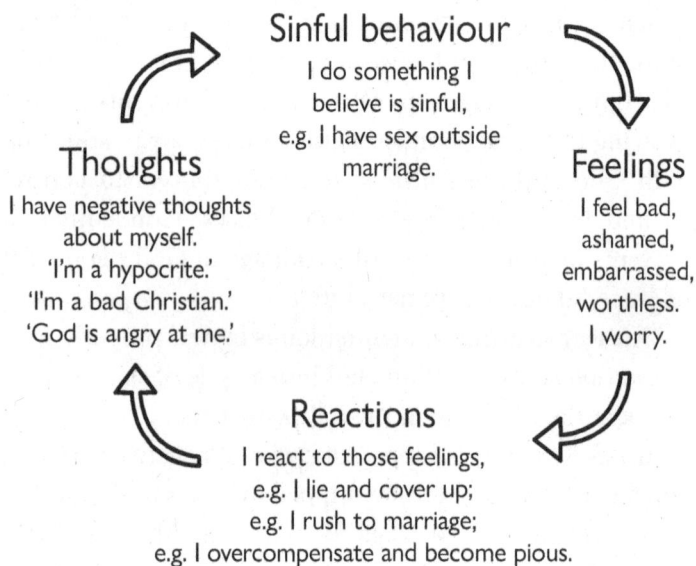

Sinful behaviour

I do something I believe is sinful, e.g. I have sex outside marriage.

Thoughts

I have negative thoughts about myself.
'I'm a hypocrite.'
'I'm a bad Christian.'
'God is angry at me.'

Feelings

I feel bad, ashamed, embarrassed, worthless. I worry.

Reactions

I react to those feelings, e.g. I lie and cover up; e.g. I rush to marriage; e.g. I overcompensate and become pious.

To consider

Can you think of any occasions when you were stuck in this cycle of shame? Or is there something you currently feel guilty about that could lead to this cycle? How can you break the cycle and respond differently in this particular situation?

Tips for dealing with guilt

- Remind yourself daily that God does not expect you to be perfect. We have all sinned and fallen short of the glory of God, and while we were still sinners, God loved us.
- If you are a parent, consider your love for your own children. Do you love them more or less when they behave well or badly? God is a perfect parent and doesn't love us any less when we sin. God just wants better for us. Believe this.
- Ask yourself whose voice you are hearing when you feel guilt. Is it the voice of someone whose opinion you trust? Or are you simply repeating the negative things abusive or unhealthy people have said to you?
- Build your relationship with God. Focus on loving God rather than simply following rules.
- When you've messed up, take responsibility for it and then remind yourself that it's dealt with. God has literally removed that sin from you. It does not define you any longer.

To do

When I was a child, I was always breaking things, often through playing silly games I shouldn't have been playing.

When I broke some of my mother's china playing football in the house, I was terrified of my father's wrath. Unlike God, my dad wasn't 'perfect' and I'm sure I probably did face some punishment. But my overarching memory is that within a few days the china was back in its place, glued back together by my dad who could fix anything.

Our heavenly Father does this with our mistakes. We can approach the throne of the King of heaven, repentant and broken, not in fear of punishment, but in full confidence that God will gently put things right. In God's eyes we are still children, growing, learning and needing to be loved and cherished. Do you treat yourself like that when you mess up?

This week, find a way to connect with the little girl you once were, because she's still there and she still needs love. What did you enjoy doing as a child? Go and do that! Perhaps get out your roller-skates or tip out the bucket of Lego; find your felt-tips or finger paints. Go and play just for the sake of playing.

In her words

I felt very guilty to begin with for taking my son away from his dad. I then realised it was my ex's actions and choices that led to the marriage breakdown, not mine.

I was ashamed of having a failed marriage and that I couldn't make it work. I am now proud that I was brave enough to get out.

(Anonymous survivor)

8

When will I stop feeling angry?

Section 1: Is anger a sin?

Such a thing has never been seen or done, not since the day the Israelites came up out of Egypt. Just imagine! We must do something! So, speak up!
(Judges 19:30, NIV)

Is anger a sin? What do you think?

Anger is morally neutral. It is neither good nor bad – it's a normal human emotion. It's how we respond to anger that matters. The Bible does not tell us to never feel anger. In fact, it assumes that we will experience anger at times, telling us not to sin when we do.

Those of us who have been abused by the person who made vows to love, protect and cherish us are right to feel angry. Domestic abuse is a huge betrayal and injustice, so it is normal and, in fact, healthy to feel angry about it.

There are several instances of Jesus expressing his anger in the gospels. Perhaps the most famous example of Jesus' anger is the story of him flipping over tables in the Temple, then driving out the con artists with a whip (Mark 11:15–18). Jesus was angry because he saw vulnerable people being exploited in a place of worship. He didn't only burn with anger for injustice done to other people though. Like the rest of us, he experienced personal anger. In Mark 11:12–25, we read that he cursed a fig tree because there was no fruit on it for him to eat. Jesus was human – he experienced the full range of human emotions and got 'hangry'. Jesus also got angry with his disciples from time to time. In Matthew 4:10, we read that he snapped at Peter, saying, 'Away with you, Satan!' These are strong words to use on one of his faithful friends and followers. Feeling anger is normal. Jesus felt anger – it is not a sin.

In chapter 19 of the book of Judges, we read about the brutal rape and dismembering of a woman. When the people of Israel saw this, they said, 'Such a thing has never been seen or done, not since the day the Israelites came up out of Egypt. Just imagine! We must do something! So speak up!' (Judges 19:30, NIV). In the end, they went to war over it. They were angry and they set out to do something about it, to put right the injustice. Violence against women is something all of God's people should be angry about. It's something God is angry about. Psalm 11:5 tells us that 'those who love violence, he hates with a passion' (NIV). Proverbs 6:16 tells us that there are six things the Lord *hates*. One of them is 'hands that shed innocent blood'. And Malachi 2:16 speaks directly about domestic violence, telling us that the Lord *hates* it when a man is violent towards the one he is supposed to protect. God is angry about domestic abuse, God hates abuse. Anyone who has a heart after God's own heart, then, should also hate abuse and should feel angry about it.

When God's people encountered the injustice of violence against a woman, their anger was a force for good, spurring them on to make a change and to right a wrong. Throughout history, angry people have changed the world. When people become angry at injustice, they take action to change it, from the abolitionists to Rosa Parks; from the suffragettes to the Stonewall riots. Anger inspires action and change, and brings about justice.

Perhaps the most important discovery humanity has ever made is fire. The consumption of cooked food led to the development of larger brains, as well as social skills. Had humanity not harnessed fire to use for warmth, deterring predators and cooking and farming food, we could have died out. Fire is essential to life. However, if left uncontrolled, fire destroys. It burns down rainforests, destroys habitats and wipes out whole species and civilisations. Anger is like fire. It's an essential force that in many circumstances protects us and keeps us safe, but if we do not learn to control it, it can also be destructive. Our anger should not be ignored or hidden away; it is not something we should feel guilty about. It is not a bad thing – it is necessary. Like fire, our anger should be embraced and harnessed. It needs to be controlled and used to become a force for good, whether that good is changing the world or protecting ourselves from future abuse.

This might be easier said than done though. I cannot begin to tell you the crazy, stupid things I did in anger when I first left my abusive husband. For me, the anger erupted because of years of denial and suppression. I had the sudden and devastating realisation that I had been experiencing deliberate manipulation and abuse. The rage was all-consuming. It would sporadically come over me in waves, impairing my ability to think clearly and make good decisions. I genuinely felt as though I were losing my mind. I allowed myself to succumb to it. As a result, I behaved in ways I regret. I misdirected anger at innocent people and, when I did choose to direct it at my ex-husband, I put myself in dangerous situations and gave him opportunities for further abuse. In the next section we will look at how you can control your anger and avoid some of the mistakes I made. If you have failed in this so far, though, please know you are not alone.

Anger is part of the experience of grieving for the losses we have experienced, and it will return again and again. In my experience, as time passed and I processed those feelings, it returned increasingly less forcefully. As I recovered, I learned to recognise the anger building, to pause before reacting, to find ways to regain my composure and ability to think clearly and, importantly, to direct it in healthy and positive ways. Eleven years later I'm still angry, but I am less angry about my own personal experience and angrier that abuse is still happening to others, and in churches at the same rates as everywhere else. I don't want to lose that anger, because if I do, I will lose the motivation to do something about it. Anger is no longer an all-consuming fire for me; it is the furnace that powers my work and spurs me on to seek justice.

To consider

Can you think of any occasions in your own life, or throughout history, when anger has been a force for good?

How can anger keep you safe from abuse?

How could your anger put you in danger of further abuse?

Has your own uncontrolled anger ever been a destructive force?

To do

If you are able to, light a fire, toast some marshmallows and enjoy watching the flames dance. There's something really lovely about sitting by a fire. If you're not able to light a fire, did you know that you can toast marshmallows over a tealight? Make yourself a nice hot drink, light some candles and relax.

Section 2: Dealing with anger

> Be angry, but do not sin; do not let the sun go down
> on your anger, and do not make room for the devil.
> (Ephesians 4:26–27)

Think of as many things as you can that make you angry.
Not just the big things like social injustices and domestic
abuse, but the smaller things too, like waiting on hold or
having to ask your children to put their shoes on twenty
million times before they do. Write them in the body of the
picture of an angry woman opposite.

Now, with a different colour pen, think about the way
anger makes you feel and add that around the body of
the picture. Think of the physical feelings, like adrenaline
coursing through your muscles, tension headaches, elevated
heartrate. What does it physically feel like to get angry?

You'll notice that the body is shaped like a bottle.
Imagine a bottle of something fizzy with a stopper in
the top. If you continually fill it and shake it up without
removing the stopper, what will happen? The build-up of
pressure will cause the stopper to explode out of the top,
and the fizzy liquid will foam up everywhere, making a
big mess.

Unexpressed anger is like that. Some Christians feel we
mustn't show our anger, but when we do not find healthy
ways to express it, our anger is likely to explode and come
spilling out in inappropriate, irrational ways – often at
the people who least deserve it. That's when anger is
destructive. In addition, if we have experienced abuse, we

When will I stop feeling angry?

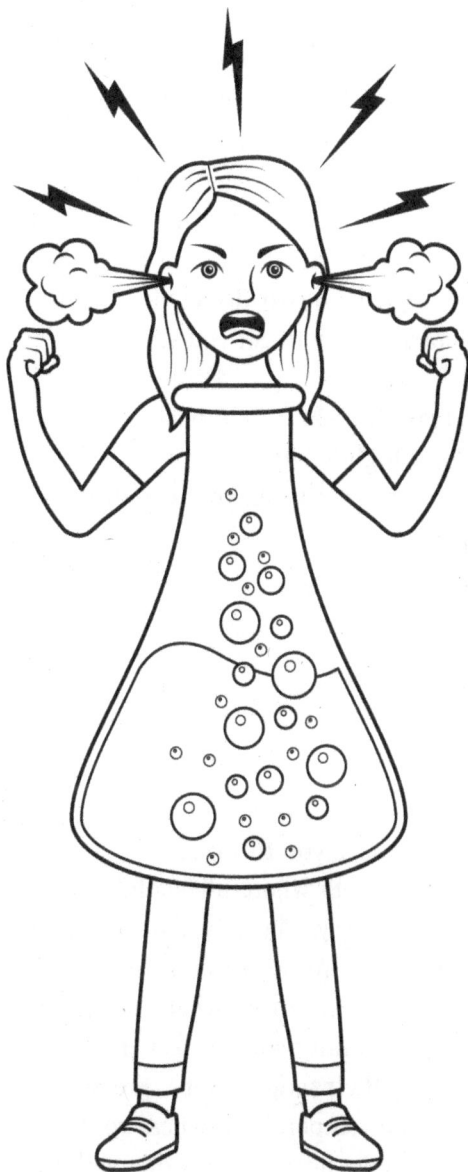

have been in situations where it was unsafe to express our anger towards the person who caused it. This can mean our anger gets misdirected towards others or that repressing it becomes a habit. It's good to find healthy ways to express our anger, but that can be easier said than done.

Round the outside of the picture, write as many things as you can think of that you might have heard when you were angry, or have heard directed towards other angry women. Here are a few to get you started:

- Don't get your knickers in a twist.
- Get off your high horse.
- You're cute/sexy/hot when you're angry.
- You're hysterical.

How many more can you think of?

We live in a society where nice ladylike women are not expected to get angry. There is a stereotype that women who express anger are out of control, insane or perhaps simply bossy. There are times when the Church feeds into this stereotype, making women feel they must always be demure, holding their tongue, not expressing opinions and never losing their temper. Even when women express their anger in reasonable, healthy ways they will hear the same insults: 'psycho', 'crazy', 'hysterical', even 'selfish' or 'demon possessed', and this leads to us repressing our anger. The problem with this is that when it does eventually spill over, we find ourselves behaving in out-of-control ways and so feeding the narrative of the hysterical woman.

We not only need strategies to express our anger in healthy ways, but we need the confidence and assertiveness to recognise when we are doing so, and not allow sexist criticism to faze us. No matter what society tells us, we have a right to be angry. We have a right to express our anger, as long as we do not do so in sinful ways that cause harm to others.

Ten tips for dealing with anger

Be prepared

Recognise that anger is a normal human emotion and there will be times when you get angry. By knowing this, you won't be as likely to be caught off guard when it happens. Plan in advance how you will deal with anger when it arises.

Practise mindfulness

Mindfulness techniques focus on noticing bodily feelings and sitting back to look at them objectively rather than reacting. Learn to notice the physical feelings of rising anger. Look at those you wrote inside the body of the diagram earlier in this section. Practise observing those feelings without response.

Do not act or make decisions while angry

When we act in the heat of the moment, we are more prone to impulsivity. We are more likely to do something we will regret. Wait until you feel calmer to make decisions.

Use assertiveness techniques

These help you to express your anger assertively; for example, by focusing on the behaviour you are angry about rather than personally attacking the person who has upset you. Or you could use the broken-record technique to calmly tell someone, 'I don't like this behaviour' – repeatedly, until they get the message.

Get out

If you are able to, remove yourself from the situation that is making you angry. If a situation, person or place regularly arouses your anger, it might be a sign that your life would be better off without them. Or perhaps you may need to remove yourself temporarily until you feel better.

Be constructive

Direct your anger constructively: start a petition, volunteer, write a letter, join a protest. It is good to seek justice. The Bible tells us to do so several times.

Find an outlet

This will look different for different people. Find the thing that works for you: it could be exercise, such as going for a run, or creativity, such as art or poetry. Or perhaps you need to hit a pillow or find a large empty space and have a good old scream!

Turn to God

Pray. Read your Bible, meditate, take it to God. You can shout at God about it if you need to. God has broad shoulders and is able to handle your frustrations, just as any good parent lovingly handles their child's frustrations. In 1 Peter 5:7 we are told, 'Cast all your anxiety on him, because he cares for you.'

Don't hide it

Express how you're feeling. It's all right to say, 'This is making me feel angry. Can we discuss it later?'

Count

Count to ten – or a hundred if you need to! Use deep-breathing or other relaxation techniques, and listen to calming or happy music to help you feel calmer.

What would you add to this list?

To consider

We will all find different ways of coping with anger. Complete the following sentences to create your own personal action plan:

- If I am feeling angry, I can go to ....
....
to help me feel better.
- The best outlet for my anger is to ....
....
- The best way for me to relax and feel calm is to ....
....
- One sentence I can use to tell people I am angry and need some space is: ....
....
- I know I can talk to God even when I am angry, because ....
- A constructive project I can start, to channel my anger, is: ....

To do

Collect some old broken crockery. In a safe space, smash the crockery up into small pieces using a hammer. Next, roll out a piece of air-drying clay to a depth of about 2 cm. Take your pieces of broken crockery and create a beautiful mosaic by pushing them into the piece of clay. Leave it to harden and then use glue to secure any loose pieces. Remind yourself that anger doesn't always have to be destructive. It can be a force for good, and even something that has been broken can be made into something beautiful.

In her words

It has taken time, but I feel I am more me now than I ever have been! I hadn't realised how, over that time, my identity had been eroded and changed into what my husband wanted me to be. It was never, ever enough though!

I have rediscovered Doc Martens and half a shaved head – definitely more me!

(Anonymous survivor)

Bible study 4

How did Jesus behave towards women?

Now there was a woman who had been suffering from haemorrhages for twelve years; and though she had spent all she had on physicians, no one could cure her. She came up behind him and touched the fringe of his clothes, and immediately her haemorrhage stopped. Then Jesus asked, 'Who touched me?' When all denied it, Peter said, 'Master, the crowds surround you and press in on you.' But Jesus said, 'Someone touched me; for I noticed that power had gone out of me.' When the woman saw that she could not remain hidden, she came trembling; and falling down before him, she declared in the presence of all the people why she had touched him, and how she had been immediately healed. He said to her, 'Daughter, your faith has made you well; go in peace.'
(Luke 8:43–48)

I remember suffering with long heavy periods when I had problems with my contraceptive implant. It was horrible. I cannot imagine how exhausting a twelve-year-long period must have been. For a Jewish woman in Jesus' time the effects were more than just physical. Leviticus 15:19–33 details the law concerning women during the time they were bleeding.

The woman who came to Jesus would have been considered permanently 'unclean'. Anything she touched was unclean, and anyone who touched not only her but anything she had touched needed to immediately bathe and change their clothes. Even so, they were still considered unclean for the rest of the day. All this meant she was completely deprived of human contact. She was not allowed to go to the Temple and not allowed to go anywhere that she could come into contact with people. Just by going out to a busy street she was breaking the law, let alone touching a rabbi.

On top of this, as well as becoming an outcast, she would have been blamed for it. At that time, ongoing medical conditions were considered a curse or punishment from God for sinful behaviour. Jesus was expected to be disgusted that she had touched him. He was expected to consider her unclean and sinful. A few verses earlier, we read that Jesus was on his way to heal the sick child of an important and wealthy man, Jairus. It would not have been considered acceptable for him to delay this by stopping to talk to an unclean woman.

To consider

When Jesus asked who had touched him, do you think he knew? If so, why did he ask?

Why did he make the woman publicly tell him she had touched him? Was he trying to humiliate her?

Who did Jesus credit with healing the woman?

What would this have meant for her within her culture?

Do you think Jesus considered her needs to be as important as those of Jairus and his daughter?

By making the woman publicly identify herself and then announcing, 'Your faith has made you well', Jesus did more than simply heal the woman. He restored her standing in the community. He made sure everyone knew that the woman they considered unclean was no longer unclean. Not only that, the reason she was healed was her own faith. Jesus could have responded to this woman the way the Pharisees would have done, by chastising her for touching a religious man and making him unclean. He could have taken full credit for curing her and used her to further enhance his own reputation. He could have assumed that what he had felt was just the crowds pressing in on him. He was rushing to the home of an important man, so it may even have been tempting to just ignore her and rush on by.

But Jesus chose, against the prevailing culture, to take time out to heal and empower this woman, treating her as an equal to the men around her, and ensuring she would no longer be ostracised.

Jesus said that he felt the power go out of him. Do you think he could have stopped this from happening, or did he make a choice to give away his power?

How does this story suggest we should use our power?

Here are some other examples of Jesus' interactions with women:

- The woman at the well (John 4:1–42).
- The woman caught in adultery (John 8:1–11).
- The woman who anointed Jesus with oil (Matthew 26:6–13; Mark 14:3–9; Luke 7:36–50; John 12:1–8).
- Mary sitting at Jesus' feet (Luke 10:38–42).

Was his treatment of women similar to that of other religious leaders of the time and if not, how was it different?

In these stories we see Jesus not only respecting women as equals, but commissioning them as important workers in his kingdom. The woman at the well is thought to have been the first evangelist. We see him protecting and defending women; challenging societal double standards about men and women; encouraging women; and challenging the notion that women should only hold domestic roles. In the story of Mary sitting at Jesus' feet, this didn't just mean she was sitting on the floor next to him. The phrase 'to sit at the feet of a teacher' meant to be a disciple. Mary was making a choice, a choice to go into the room with the men, not to serve them as would have been expected, but to join them as a disciple of Jesus, and Jesus said that in doing so she had 'made the better choice'.

Jesus never expected women to stay in the home. He never saw women as objects only for sex and service. He treated women as fully human and fully equal in worth and role to men. Who were the first people to see the risen Christ and tell everyone the good news? Women.

What do these stories mean for you in your relationship with Jesus? Do you identify with any particular woman from these stories, or is there a particular story of Jesus' treatment of women that really stands out to you?

In her words

My abuse had roots in my belief that my relationship with God didn't matter and so I didn't matter. It had never occurred to me that anyone could be curious about my inner life, let alone be respectful of it. Jesus seeking out the story, honouring the faith and recognising the woman [in Luke 8:43–48] as part of his family shows me that I matter to God and my beliefs are crucial to the quality of my life. This is literally life-changing.

(Anonymous survivor)

My notes

My notes

9

What about forgiveness?

Section 1: Forgiveness and reconciliation

> Then Peter came and said to him, 'Lord, if another
> member of the church sins against me, how often
> should I forgive? As many as seven times?' Jesus said
> to him, 'Not seven times, but, I tell you, seventy-seven
> times.'
> (Matthew 18:21–22)

Have you been urged to do your Christian duty and forgive
your abuser? Or have you put pressure on yourself to
forgive? You've probably read this verse, maybe even had it
quoted at you to urge you to 'forgive and forget'.

Some translations don't say 'seventy-seven times'; they
say 'seventy times seven times'. I'm not good at maths but
I know that seventy times seven is significantly more than
seventy-seven. The number here isn't important; it's not
the point. The point is that the Old Testament laws gave a
number: an Israelite was expected to forgive seven times,
and seven times only. Jesus, however, went further, telling
us to just keep on forgiving. There's no way around it.
Forgiveness is a big deal in the Christian faith.

The average woman will leave and then return to her
abusive partner eight times before she leaves for good.
This sometimes makes me wonder if the ancient Israelites

had the better idea: seven times is enough. If behaviour doesn't change after seven times, it's time to say enough is enough. Jesus' command to forgive seems to run counter to safety advice, which would tell us not to keep returning to people who put us in danger. This is one reason that many Christian women do not leave abusive relationships for a long time. We want to keep on forgiving, time after time. We believe forgiveness should have no limits. Hence we become doormats, continually forgiving the same behaviour over and over again while nothing changes.

Many of us will have felt pressure from our husbands, our churches or our communities to stay in abusive relationships because of the Christian directive to forgive. This is a poor understanding of forgiveness. We are told to forgive but not necessarily to reconcile. Reconciliation can only occur where there is both repentance and forgiveness. When there has been no repentance, reconciliation is ill advised, because without repentance nothing changes and the behaviour continues. When this behaviour is abusive, we are putting ourselves in more danger each time we return. This is why Jesus says that we should *forgive* seventy-seven times, not that we should *reconcile* seventy-seven times. When there has been abuse, it is important to put safety ahead of reconciliation. Refusal to reconcile does not mean refusal to forgive. It is perfectly possible to leave an abusive marriage and to forgive the abuser at the same time.

I would go further to suggest that the forgiveness we offer when we reconcile with those who continue to abuse us is not real biblical forgiveness. When we remain in an abusive relationship, it is necessary for our sanity and our survival to minimise or deny the abuse. We tell ourselves that it's not really abuse, or it's not that bad. We tell ourselves that this isn't the 'real him'; that he cannot really help it, he didn't mean to or he's trying his best to change. In order to forgive the hurt we have been caused, we have to first acknowledge and fully understand what has been done to us. We don't do that when we stay, deny and minimise. Therefore, we cannot fully forgive, because we don't fully acknowledge the need for forgiveness in the first place. We don't fully acknowledge the magnitude of the sin.

When we return, this is not forgiving; it is forgetting. We offer a weaker version of forgiveness. This imitation of forgiveness means we do not experience the lifting of the burden of their sin, or the heart-changing gift of releasing another person's debt to us. We cannot, because we don't even recognise that they have that debt to us in the first place. Forgiveness is difficult; to properly and fully forgive we need power and strength. Abuse strips us of our power; it weakens us. It not only takes away our recognition of the magnitude of forgiveness required, but it also takes away the tools we need to be able to forgive.

What is forgiveness?

Let's start by looking at the rest of the passage in Matthew 18, after Peter had asked Jesus how many times he should forgive his brother:

'For this reason, the kingdom of heaven may be compared to a king who wished to settle accounts

with his slaves. When he began the reckoning, one who owed him ten thousand talents was brought to him; and, as he could not pay, his lord ordered him to be sold, together with his wife and children and all his possessions, and payment to be made. So the slave fell on his knees before him, saying, "Have patience with me and I will pay you everything." And out of pity for him, the lord of that slave released him and forgave him the debt. But that same slave, as he went out, came upon one of his fellow-slaves who owed him a hundred denarii, and seizing him by the throat, he said, "Pay what you owe." Then his fellow-slave fell down and pleaded with him, "Have patience with me and I will pay you." But he refused; then he went and threw him into prison until he should pay the debt. When his fellow-slaves saw what had happened, they were greatly distressed, and they went and reported to their lord all that had taken place. Then his lord summoned him and said to him, "You wicked slave! I forgave you all that debt because you pleaded with me. Should you not have had mercy on your fellow-slave, as I had mercy on you?" And in anger his lord handed him over to be tortured until he would pay his entire debt.'
(Matthew 18:23–34)

Forgiveness is the cancellation of debts – not just financial but anything you may feel is owed to you. At the end of a relationship, particularly one where we have been hurt, we can feel cheated. We've invested not only money but time and emotions, hopes and dreams in the other person. It's natural to feel we are owed those things, and while they cannot be repaid, seeing that person hurt, suffer or fail can feel a bit like a repayment. I remember when I first left my abusive husband, I listened to the Faith Hill song 'Cry' and identified with the lyrics. In the song a woman is asking her ex to cry. She says that if he felt bad, it would make her feel better about the pain he caused. She feels she is owed his pain in return for everything he has taken from her. She says she doesn't want him to pity her; she just wants him to feel the pain he has caused to her.

Remember all those tears that God collects in his jar? That's what we're owed by our abusers. They owe us an emotional debt, and it's one that can never, and will never, be repaid. Forgiveness is letting go of that debt. Letting go of the desire for it to be repaid through the other person's pain and suffering. That's not easy, is it? In fact, I think it might be more difficult than reconciliation.

To consider

What is the thing you find most difficult to forgive?

Does the notion of forgiveness as releasing an emotional debt resonate with you? If not, what does forgiveness mean to you?

Is it possible to forgive without having contact with the person you are forgiving?

How will you know you have forgiven your abuser?

Do you want to forgive your abuser?

To do

Are there any songs that emotionally resonate with you, or that make you feel better when you're down? See if you can create an empowering playlist of feel-good music that you can listen to whenever you need a pick-me-up. Here are a few of mine to get you started:

- 'These Boots Are Made for Walkin'' by Nancy Sinatra
- 'Shake It Off' by Taylor Swift
- 'Shout Out to My Ex' by Little Mix.

Section 2: What if I don't want to forgive?

Put away from you all bitterness and wrath and anger and wrangling and slander, together with all malice, and be kind to one another, tender-hearted, forgiving one another, as God in Christ has forgiven you.
(Ephesians 4:31–32)

On 23 August 1973 a thief named Jan-Erik Olsson tried to rob a bank in Stockholm. Taking four people hostage, he demanded that his former cellmate Clark Olofsson be released from prison and brought to the bank. Between them, the two men held the four people for six days. When the hostages were finally released, none of them would testify against their captors. They even started raising money for Olsson and Olofsson's legal defence. One hostage told news reporters that she did not fear her captors but feared the police. This is where the term 'Stockholm syndrome' comes from.

When we experience trauma, it creates a need for emotional attachment. When we are in abusive situations we form that emotional attachment to our abusers. This is particularly likely to happen if we experience the cycle of violence that we looked at in chapter 1. The fear we feel during the abuse stage of the cycle is replaced by gratitude during the honeymoon stage. As we normalise the abusive behaviour, we begin to see our abuser's occasional acts of kindness as extraordinary love, so we form much stronger traumatic attachments. This is why we often feel such

strong feelings of love for our abuser. It's why it may feel that we have a remarkably deep connection that others don't understand. In some cases, this means that we don't feel we have any difficulty in forgiving our abuser, because we still love him.

Just like the forgiveness we offer when we return, this is not the real deep biblical forgiveness that Jesus was telling us is essential. This is because we're still not seeing our abuser for who he is. He is someone who has made a deliberate choice to exert power and control over us. He is someone who has failed to treat us with the love we deserve. He is someone who does not deserve our forgiveness. Forgiveness is remarkable, because it is wholly undeserved. In order to reach a stage where we can truly forgive, we have to deal with any trauma bonds that may make us feel that we are still in love with our abuser.

When we know that the man we love is a dangerous abuser, it can feel incredibly confusing. Our head tells us that we need to flee, but our heart keeps pulling us back. Imagine you are attached to your abuser with a bungee cord – every time you pull away, it pulls you back. Now imagine you have a small pair of scissors. You'll find it is almost impossible to cut through a thick bungee cord with scissors. Almost. Bungee cords are made up of hundreds of thinner individual elastic cords, so with your scissors you can cut through one cord at a time. It may take a long time, you may get pulled back as you are doing so, but eventually you will be free. Working at your recovery one step at a time means reminding yourself of the harm that's been done to you and leaning into those healthy feelings of anger. When you do this, you will eventually reach a place where you are no longer in love with your abuser. This is when real forgiveness starts to become an option. It's also when you're less likely to want to offer it.

Many of us find that when we lean into our anger and contemplate the hurt caused to us, those strong feelings of love are replaced by hatred. As Christians we are taught not to hate, but to put aside all bitterness and forgive. If we're in a stage of hating our abuser, we might feel that we are being sinful, that we are failing as Christians. If this is the case it may be an idea to revisit the chapter on guilt.

The Bible is right – if we remain in our anger and hatred it turns to bitterness. This is not good for us. However, the Bible also tells us that there is a season for everything. It even says that there is 'a time to love, and a time to hate' (Ecclesiastes 3:8). Feeling hatred for someone who has abused you is normal, and for a period of time it is healthy. It protects you from returning to that situation. It may spur you to seek justice through the legal system, or to protect your children through the family court. There will be a time when you need that hatred, to keep you safe and, essentially, to help you recognise the seriousness of what you have been through.

Are you at a point where you hate him and cannot contemplate forgiving him? That's OK. This is all part of the recovery process, and it takes time.

To consider

What are the benefits of forgiveness?

Who benefits from your forgiveness?

Why does Jesus tell us to forgive?

Is it a sin not to forgive?

Forgiveness is a good thing when it is real and genuine, and the time is right for it, but it is not a process that can be forced or rushed. You cannot be guilted into forgiving. When we forgive, it releases us from the emotional burden that abuse causes. It prevents us from becoming bitter and gives us the opportunity to move on. Our abuser doesn't care if we forgive him or not – the majority of abusers don't even believe they *need* to be forgiven. They reap no benefits from our forgiveness; the benefits are all ours. This is why Jesus wants us to forgive. It is good for us, and any good parent wants what's best for their child.

In the previous section of this chapter, we looked at Matthew 18 and stopped at verse 34: 'And in anger his lord handed him over to be tortured until he should pay his entire debt.' Verse 35 continues: 'So my heavenly Father will also do to every one of you, if you do not forgive your brother or sister from your heart.'

Sounds scary, doesn't it? You may have even been told that you must forgive or you won't be forgiven. I don't believe God is so cruel. This story relates to behaviour, not feelings. The slave in the story had the person who owed him thrown in jail; he sought vengeance. Whether or not we have reached the point emotionally where we can release the desire to see the other person suffer, we can all choose the loving course of action. We may feel utter hatred for our abuser, but we can choose not to seek out ways to harm or hurt him. We can choose to act with grace and agape love, even if we are seething with hatred. This is the action of loving our enemies. It is our behaviour that matters here – not what we feel, but how we respond to our feelings.

I am certain God would be unhappy should we choose to seek vengeance or cause harm to those who have hurt us. That is a sin. But struggling with our feelings towards them, feeling anger, hatred, and being unable to reach a point where we can categorically say we have forgiven them is not the same. I don't believe God would be angry with us for that. God wants to help us navigate those big feelings and that part of our recovery – in all the time we need.

To do

Consider where you are on your recovery journey and your feelings towards the person who hurt you. Are you still feeling love, or hatred, or have you reached apathy, where you don't really feel anything for them? Do you struggle with forgiveness? If so, take it to God. It's OK to tell God where you are struggling. It's even OK to tell God if you don't want to forgive. The Psalms are full of prayers asking God to smite the psalmist's enemies. Those feelings are legitimate. Take your feelings to God and try writing your own psalm about your journey with forgiveness and what you need from God.

In her words

I was referred by my Relate counsellor to our local domestic abuse charity. I went along thinking that they would laugh at my story and tell me not to waste their time. Instead, they recommended weekly sessions, the Freedom Programme, and counselling for my son. This was such a shock, as I had minimised the extent of the emotional neglect and control.

I was constantly told by my ex it was my fault, and I believed it must have been something I'd done or not done. As I admitted to what had really been happening, I went through the whole range of emotions: anger at myself and at my ex, shame that I'd put up with it for so long, resentment, relief, anxiety about the future, to name a few!

I realised forgiveness wasn't about going back to the marriage. Forgiveness was saying, 'The way you treated me was wrong. I forgive you for that, but that doesn't mean I have to live with you and do what you say.'

(Anonymous survivor)

Bible study 5

What does God think of divorce?

You ask, 'Why does he not?' Because the LORD was a witness between you and the wife of your youth, to whom you have been faithless, though she is your companion and your wife by covenant. Did not one God make her? Both flesh and spirit are his. And what does the one God desire? Godly offspring. So look to yourselves, and do not let anyone be faithless to the wife of his youth. For I hate divorce, says the LORD, the God of Israel, and covering one's garment with violence, says the LORD of hosts. So take heed to yourselves and do not be faithless.
(Malachi 2:14–16)

How might these verses be interpreted to make life more difficult for women in abusive relationships?

It's around 400 years before the birth of Jesus. God's people in Israel have been through a lot, but now things should be looking up. They've returned to Jerusalem from exile in Babylon, have rebuilt the Temple and are now able to re-establish their culture and faith in their homeland. But Malachi isn't happy. His book laments that the current generation of Israelites is just as corrupt and faithless as the previous ones and, as a result, Malachi sees injustice all around him.

In that context he writes these verses. Who are the verses addressed to and what were they doing wrong?

These verses are addressed to men. We know this because Malachi refers to 'your wife'. From reading the books of Ezra and Nehemiah we learn that Israelite men were abandoning their wives to marry women from other cultures. In 430 BC women could not enter into a contract. This meant that while in theory they could divorce their husbands, in practical terms it was almost impossible for them to do so, because they would need a man to help them. Men, however, could instigate divorce for any reason they liked.

Divorce was particularly unjust for women, because divorced women were no longer virgins and thus were considered 'spoiled goods' – not suitable for marriage. Women who were unmarried had to rely on male relatives to care for them. If they did not have male relatives who were willing to take them in, they became destitute, with prostitution often their only means of survival. When men were divorcing their wives to marry younger foreign women, they were subjecting their former wives to a life of destitution or prostitution. No wonder Malachi was lamenting the injustices he saw around him.

In the first Bible study, we looked at the importance of understanding the spirit of the law rather than simply following the law without considering love. To understand the spirit of the law we need to consider why the rule has been put in place. God's hatred of divorce, and the subsequent rules cautioning against divorce, existed to protect women from being left destitute by men who simply wanted to trade them in for a younger model. In biblical times divorce was a form of violence against women.

In Matthew 19 we read a similar condemnation of divorce from Jesus:

> Some Pharisees came to him, and to test him they asked, 'Is it lawful for a man to divorce his wife for any cause?' He answered, 'Have you not read that the one who made them at the beginning "made them male and female", and said, "For this reason a man shall leave his father and mother and be joined to his wife, and the two shall become one flesh"? So they are no longer two, but one flesh. Therefore, what God has joined together, let no one separate.' They said

to him, 'Why then did Moses command us to give a certificate of dismissal and to divorce her?' He said to them, 'It was because you were so hard-hearted that Moses allowed you to divorce your wives, but at the beginning it was not so. And I say to you, whoever divorces his wife, except for unchastity, and marries another commits adultery.'
(Matthew 19:3–9)

Again, we see that these words about divorce are addressed only to men. Jesus, like Malachi, is concerned with the treatment of women, and the injustice of divorce towards women at the time. Jesus reiterates the story of creation, reminding them that, in marriage, two become one flesh. This is the reason why men should not simply discard their wives as though they are an object they have grown bored with. In Genesis 2, when God creates Eve, we read, 'Then the man said, "'This at last is bone of my bones and flesh of my flesh..."' Therefore a man leaves his father and his mother and clings to his wife, and they become one flesh' (Genesis 2:23–24). Adam's declaration that Eve is 'bone of my bones and flesh of my flesh' is a declaration of her sameness. He's saying, 'This one is like me; this one is human too.' It's our shared humanity that is the reason for marriage, our equality, and it is this equality that is the root of our unity.

Jesus appeals to this 'oneness' when he tells men not to divorce their wives. He tells men to remember that women are human too; that we are equals and thus deserve to be treated with respect.

Both Jesus and Malachi spoke against divorce in order to protect women. When their words are used to trap women in dangerous and abusive marriages, this is the polar opposite of what they were intended to do. The spirit of the Bible's teachings on divorce was the protection of women. Today, the safest thing for a woman to do may be to get a divorce.

To consider

In Malachi 2:16 why does it say that the Lord hates divorce?

What behaviour was God condemning in this passage?

Why do you think God commanded men not to divorce their wives?

When Jesus later prohibited divorce, who was he protecting?

What is God's intention in both of these passages? What is the spirit of the law here?

Verse 16 tells us that God hates not only divorce but also 'covering one's garment with violence'. In the NIV translation this reads, 'does violence to the one he should protect'. The differences in versions can make this a tricky verse to translate. In her book *The Bible Doesn't Tell Me So*, the Revd Dr Helen Paynter suggests that to cover one's garment in violence may be referring to the marriage custom of the day, where a man appears to have taken the woman under his cloak as a sign of her entering his protection... Malachi is referring to the bringing of violence into the marital home. This constitutes a breach of the marriage covenant.[23]

What does Malachi 2:16 tell us about God's attitude to domestic abuse?

Do we read at any point that God hates divorcees?

---

23 Helen Paynter, *The Bible Doesn't Tell Me So: Why you don't have to submit to domestic abuse and coercive control* (Abingdon: BRF, 2020).

In her words

God reminded me so many times, 'I've got you . . . you've got this', especially through refuge and family court.

(Anonymous survivor)

My notes

My notes

10

A new future

Section 1: Rights, responsibilities and singleness

'Come to me, all you that are weary and carrying heavy burdens, and I will give you rest. Take my yoke upon you, and learn from me; for I am gentle and humble in heart, and you will find rest for your souls. For my yoke is easy, and my burden is light.'
(Matthew 11:28–30)

I hope that as you've worked through this book you have seen yourself as God sees you: as a beloved masterpiece of creation, a daughter of the King of kings, worthy of love and respect. In order to keep ourselves safe within an abusive relationship, we may have had to give up on the idea of enjoying the rights that are afforded to a daughter of the King of kings. We may have written off things like the right to be loved and respected, or the right to live free from fear. When we escape the abuse, it can take some time to recognise that we are humans of worth, with inalienable human rights.

On the next page you will see a 'bill of rights'. Have a think about what your rights as a human are. Not your legal or constitutional rights, but the things you should be able to expect in the way you are treated by others. There are a few already on there to get you started, so add some of your own.

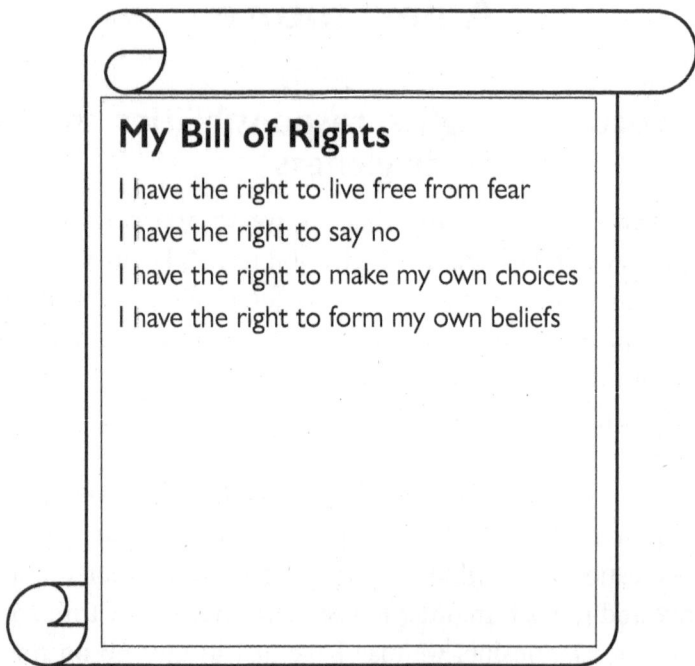

My Bill of Rights

I have the right to live free from fear
I have the right to say no
I have the right to make my own choices
I have the right to form my own beliefs

It is important to recognise our rights, because this can keep us safe in future. If we are aware of our rights and able to draw the boundaries necessary to protect them, then we are more likely to notice when they are breached. Behaviour that attempts to undermine our rights can serve as a red flag in any future potential relationship.

A red flag is something that sets off alarm bells about a person's behaviour. Now that we have a good understanding of what abuse looks like, there are red flags or early warning signs we can spot that might be a sign someone is likely to use abusive behaviours.

Have a think about the abusive behaviours we looked at earlier from 1 Corinthians 13. For each one, see if you can think of how someone who is likely to go on to use those behaviours might behave at the start of a relationship.

Envious

Boastful

Arrogant

Rude

Selfish

Irritable

Resentful

Rejoices in wrongdoing

Here are a few red flags to watch out for. Did you get these?

- He questions my whereabouts and wants to know where I am all the time.
- He turns up with no warning under the guise of offering me a lift or romantically surprising me.
- He speaks down to waitresses/waiters/bar staff.
- He orders for me at restaurants.
- He pushes my boundaries in subtle ways, such as trying to convince me to eat food I don't like or do sexual things I don't want to.

- He buys me expensive gifts very early on and showers me with 'love'. (This is called love bombing.)
- He makes declarations of love very early on or rushes to commitment, such as living together or getting engaged.
- He uses backhanded compliments like 'You look slimmer in that dress', or 'You scrub up well'.
- He has 'mini sulks' or gets moody.
- He wants to be with me, on our own, all the time and may do things like turn up with tickets for somewhere romantic when he knows I have planned a night out with my friends.
- He tries to convince me not to go to work, college, church or out with friends: 'Pretend you're sick and let's spend the day together. It'll be romantic.'
- He tells me sob stories very early on.
- He speaks badly about his ex.
- He doesn't see his children.
- He is rigid in his doctrines and won't agree to disagree, arguing until I agree with him.
- When I have been with him, I don't feel good about myself.

Some of these are red flags you will keep an eye on, watching future behaviour carefully. Others you may consider deal breakers; you will walk away from a potential relationship straight away if you see them. This will depend on your own experiences and boundaries.

As well as understanding our rights and what red flags look like, we can also keep ourselves safe in relationships, both romantic and platonic, by understanding what our responsibilities are. You made a bill of rights, now consider below what your responsibilities are:

When we are in an abusive relationship, we are often convinced by our abuser that we are responsible for his behaviour. We might try to change ourselves or might find ourselves apologising for him. He may have made us feel as though we were responsible for his well-being. Perhaps he would 'forget' to eat or shower without us reminding him, or we believed we could fix him. Or perhaps we came to depend on him for our happiness and well-being. Society teaches little girls that once they find their Prince Charming, they will live happily ever after. We are encouraged to put the keys to our happiness in the pockets of our husbands.

We should only be responsible for our own happiness and well-being. We are responsible for setting our own boundaries and asserting our own rights, for picking ourselves up when we are down, even if it's not our fault we are down. We do not need to depend on others to make us happy and we certainly don't have the power to change another person's behaviour or to make them happy. We are only responsible for ourselves and, to an extent, for our children, if we have any. If we spend our lives focusing on the things we don't have control over, then we don't have enough time and energy to deal with the things we do.

Finally, before embarking on any new relationships, it's good to revisit the tips for setting boundaries in chapter 6 (section 2). Boundaries are not just about saying no to unacceptable behaviour. They are also about protecting our identity by recognising where the other person ends and we begin. Many of us in an abusive relationship become an extension of our partner rather than having an identity of our own. We may even have given up our whole name and just become 'the missus'. This is why, when the relationship ends, we can feel a sense of not even knowing who we are any more. It is important to be a whole person outside of our relationships. This is why it's good to spend time getting to know who you are and becoming comfortable with your own company before embarking on a relationship with someone else.

To consider

How much do you really believe, deep down, that you are entitled to the rights you wrote on your 'bill of rights'?

What are your deal breakers for a future relationship?

Do you know who you are? Do you enjoy your own company?

How will you know if you are ready to be in a new relationship?

While we have considered how to make sure future relationships are healthy and abuse-free, it is also worth pointing out that there is no requirement for anyone to be in a romantic relationship. Sometimes the Church can be guilty of making single people feel as though they have somehow failed and need to couple up, but this is categorically untrue. In fact, the apostle Paul wrote that it was good to be single (1 Corinthians 7:8). What do you think are the benefits to being single?

It's not just the Bible that says there are benefits to being single. Scientific research also points to the perks of singleness.[24] Single people tend to have stronger social networks. In 2015, social scientists Natalia Sarkisian and Noami Gerstel set out to explore how ties to family, friends and community varied among single and married Americans. They found that single people were more likely to reach out frequently to their social networks and that they also tended to give and receive help from those networks more than married people.[25]

24 Erin Brodwin, 'It's better to be single, according to science', *Independent*, 10 February 2018 at: https://www.independent.co.uk/life-style/love-sex/why-single-is-better-according-to-science-a8204476.html (accessed 27 November 2024).

25 N. Sarkisian and N. Gerstel, 'Does singlehood isolate or integrate? Examining the link between marital status and ties to kin, friends, and neighbors', 2016, *Journal of Social and Personal Relationships, 33*(3).

Single people tend to be fitter too. In surveying more than 13,000 people aged eighteen to sixty-four, researchers found that those who were single and had never married worked out more frequently than their married peers.[26]

Single people also benefit from alone time that improves their personal development. Several studies have linked solitude to an increased sense of freedom and higher levels of creativity and intimacy. Psychotherapist Amy Morin says that alone time can help people to be more productive: 'Time alone doesn't have to be lonely . . . it could be the key to getting to know yourself better.'[27] There is evidence that single people have stronger feelings of self-determination and are more likely to experience psychological growth than their married counterparts.

What do you like about being single?

There are benefits to being single and benefits to being in a relationship. The key to being content is to focus on

26 K. M. Nomaguchi and S. M. Bianchi, 'Exercise Time: Gender differences in the effects of marriage, parenthood, and employment', 2004, *Journal of Marriage and Family*, 66(2).

27 Amy Morin, cited in S. Benna, '7 ways mentally strong people take advantage of solitude' (24 July 2015) at: https://www.businessinsider.com/how-mentally-strong-people-use-solitude-2015-7 (accessed 27 November 2024).

the benefits of whichever lifestyle you lead, rather than wondering if the grass is greener on the other side. It's not greener; it's just different.

To do

Spend some time in solitude. If you can, head to a beach. If you can't, pick a forest or a quiet park instead. Breathe in the fresh air and enjoy the silence. Pray or just enjoy the peace of your own thoughts.

While you're there, find a pebble or stone – one that fits nicely into the palm of your hand. As you walk along, enjoy the feel of the pebble, its smoothness in your hand and the weight of it. Keep that pebble and use it to ground yourself whenever you need to.

Section 2: Reflection

For surely I know the plans I have for you, says the
LORD, plans for your welfare and not for harm, to give
you a future with hope.
(Jeremiah 29:11)

Whether you begin a new, healthy relationship or remain
single, the most important relationship in your life is your
relationship with God. How do you relate to God?

God created us all uniquely and, as such, every relationship
with God will be different. Yet sometimes we feel there is
a right way and perhaps even a wrong way to be in that
relationship. We tend to compare ourselves to others in
the way we worship. Perhaps some people find it easy to
spend time alone in prayer, whereas when you sit down for
a quiet time you have a habit of falling asleep. Or perhaps
someone else is really good at serving at church, but you
are socially awkward or just struggle to juggle your time.
Some find they feel God's presence in ritual; others don't.
There are as many ways of being with God as there are
humans. We don't all have to do the same things. If you're

not really a reader you might struggle to read your Bible, but you may sing and enjoy relating to God that way. We often worry about the things we don't do and forget that as long as we are spending time with God that's what counts. God is omnipresent. If you don't manage to get your quiet time with God in the morning, it's nothing to worry about. You can talk to God on the way to work. It's OK to find God in the reassuring hug you give your child or the conversation you have with another mother on the playground, or the encouragement you give a colleague or the smile you give the cashier at the supermarket. We can be in God's presence at all times – in our doing, in our very being, constantly, if that works better than having a formal routine. The important thing is to find what works for you.

I'm a doer. When I do manage to sit still, I tend to fall asleep. I have spent years feeling guilty for either not setting enough time aside to pray or falling asleep when I do. God, however, is a loving parent. I know that when my children climb up onto the sofa next to me and fall asleep with me, I love it. I love that they feel safe and comfortable in my presence. I love that they are getting what they need. When Elijah fled into the wilderness from Jezebel, God sent an angel to provide him with food, drink and rest (1 Kings 19:5–9). Being in God's presence is a balm, a time of refreshment, and if what we need is sleep, I don't think we should feel guilty about that. I know that in my best, most comfortable, human relationships some of the nicest times have been when we haven't had to talk. We've just sat quietly in each other's company. Prayer doesn't need to be full of eloquent words; it doesn't need to be scheduled time.

It's part of a dynamic, living relationship and if it takes place as you go about your life, that's OK too.

I've learned I relate best to God through action. I pray as I am doing things. I find writing works as prayer for me, but it took me a long time to learn that this is OK. Daily stillness isn't something that necessarily helps me connect with God. The important thing is knowing how you relate to God and building time for that specific thing into your schedule. I find being outside nourishes my soul, so I set aside time to write on a beach or in my campervan from time to time. That's where I am most likely to meet with God.

To consider

Where and when do you mostly notice God's presence?

How do you prefer to spend time with God?

What's the biggest obstacle to your faith?

What is your priority in your relationship with God?

Is there something you have learned about your relationship with God while reading this book?

Now would be a good time to consider how far you have come in your recovery. The journey of recovery is not like travelling down a straight, well-laid, empty road from point A to point B. It's more like trekking through the countryside on an undulating and winding path. There will be times when you feel it's more of an uphill slog. There will be times when you feel as though you are going round in circles or back on yourself. You may get stuck in mud from time to time, or just have to sit down by the side of the road and rest. No two people's recovery journey will look the same, but as long as you're on that road, putting one foot in front of the other, things will begin to look more hopeful.

Sometimes, when we're slowly ploughing uphill it can be easy to forget how far we've come. Journalling can help – we can look back on where we've been and remind ourselves how well we're doing. We can also use tools like the questions in the introduction to this book. Answer them again now, then look back at how you answered them before and compare.

Think about each of these areas and give it a score out of 10 based on how you think it's going. Then add the scores together to give yourself an overall total out of 90 (or 80 if you don't have children).

Education, work and learning ☐
Support networks and relationships ☐
Health and well-being ☐
Happiness levels ☐
My spiritual life/relationship with God ☐
Feeling safe from abuse ☐
Finances ☐
Confidence and self-esteem ☐
My ability to parent my children well (if relevant) ☐

Total score: ☐

You can also complete the self-esteem questionnaire from chapter 5 (section 2) again and compare that to last time.

A new future

	Strongly agree	Agree	Disagree	Strongly disagree
I feel that I am a person worthy of God's love	3	2	1	0
I feel I am a unique contributor of God's kingdom with a number of good qualities	3	2	1	0
All in all I am inclined to feel I have let God down	0	1	2	3
I am able to endure all things in Christ's strength	3	2	1	0
I feel I do not have much to be proud of	0	1	2	3
I take a positive attitude towards myself	3	2	1	0
On the whole I think God is pleased and proud of me	3	2	1	0
I wish I could have more respect for myself	0	1	2	3
I certainly feel useless at times	0	1	2	3
At times I feel I have much to be ashamed of	0	1	2	3

To do

Give yourself a 'word of the year'. Think of one word that you will focus on for the next twelve months. It could be a word that sums up your hopes and dreams for this year, or it could be something you want to be known for or a positive affirmation you want to remind yourself of.

Now take the pebble you collected in the last 'To do' and decorate it. Write that word on it. You could put the pebble by your bed or in your handbag or pocket. Perhaps you could put it on your desk at work. Just make sure it goes somewhere you will see it regularly and be reminded of and inspired by your word of the year.

In her words

I now have a grateful heart for all that God has done for me. I have a hope of heaven, and I live each day with the Lord, asking that I would become more righteous. I am grateful for small things and the 'little world' that I live in. I live on low earnings, but I can make it stretch.

And the verses in Habakkuk are fantastic: 'Though the fig-tree does not bud and there are no grapes on the vines, though the olive crop fails, and the fields produce no food, though there are no sheep in the pen and no cattle in the stalls, yet I will rejoice in the LORD, I will be joyful in God my Saviour. The Sovereign LORD is my strength; he makes my feet like the feet of a deer, he enables me to tread on the heights' (Habakkuk 3:17–19, NIV).
(Anonymous survivor)

May you go on to tread on the heights and live an abundant life filled with the hope of Jesus!

Bibliography and recommended reading

Carver, Joseph M., 'Love and Stockholm Syndrome: The Mystery of Loving an Abuser' (article, 25 April 2011) at: https://counsellingresource.com/therapy/self-help/stockholm

Held Evans, Rachel, 'Aristotle vs Jesus: What Makes the New Testament Household Codes Different?' (blog, 28 August 2013) at: https://rachelheldevans.com/blog/aristotle-vs-jesus-what-makes-the-new-testament-household-codes-different

Sacks, Jonathan, 'Why Storytelling is Essential to Jews and Judaism' (article, 28 January 2020) at: https://www.algemeiner.com/2020/01/28/why-storytelling-is-essential-to-jews-and-judaism/

Bancroft, Lundy, *Why Does He Do That? Inside the minds of angry and controlling men* (Berkley Publishing Group, 2002).

Barr, Beth Allison, *The Making of Biblical Womanhood* (Brazos Press, 2021).

Bates, Laura, *Everyday Sexism* (Simon and Schuster, 2015).

Bessey, Sarah, *Jesus Feminist: An invitation to revisit the Bible's view of women* (Howard Books, 2013).

Bolz-Weber, Nadia, *Shameless: A sexual reformation* (Canterbury Press, 2019).

Cosgrove S. et al., *Power to Change* (Possum Ltd, 2008).

Covey, Stephen, *The 7 Habits of Highly Effective People* (Simon & Schuster, 2013).

Craven, Pat, *Living with the Dominator* (CreateSpace Independent Publishing Platform, 2008).

Held Evans, Rachel, *A Year of Biblical Womanhood* (Nelson Books, 2012).

Herman, Judith L., *Trauma and Recovery* (Basic Books, 1992).

James, Carolyn C., *Half the Church: Recapturing God's global vision for women* (Zondervan, 2011).

Moran, Caitlin, *How to be a woman* (Ebury Press, 2012).

Pavlovitz, John, *A Bigger Table* (Westminster John Knox Press, 2017).

Paynter, Helen, *The Bible doesn't tell me so: Why you don't have to submit to domestic abuse and coercive control* (BRF, 2020).

Penna, Sue, *The Recovery Toolkit:A twelve-week plan to support your journey from Domestic Abuse* (Sue Penna Associates, 2020).

Peppiatt, Lucy, *Rediscovering Scripture's Vision for Women* (IVP Academic, 2019).

Storkey, Elaine, *Scars Across Humanity: Understanding and overcoming violence against woman* (SPCK, 2015).

Storkey, Elaine, *Women in a Patriarchal World: Twenty-five empowering stories from the Bible* (SPCK, 2020).

Sweetman, Esther (ed.), *Restored: A handbook for female Christian survivors of domestic violence* (Restored, 2019).

Tutu, Desmond and Mpho Tutu, *The Book of Forgiving* (HarperOne, 2014).

Walker, Lenore E., *The Battered Woman* (Harper and Row, 1979).

Websites

www.womensaid.org.uk
www.womankind.org.uk
www.restored-uk.org
www.theduluthmodel.org
www.hurrahforgin.com
www.ficm.org.uk

If you have found this book useful, you might also enjoy Sally Hope's other book: *30 Steps to Finding Yourself: An interactive journey to self-discovery* (Vie, 2024). You can buy it from all major bookstores or directly from Sally Hope via her website: www.alwayshopeful.org.uk

You can also connect with Sally on Facebook: facebook.com/sallyhopealwayshopeful/